Humboldt, Worldview and Language

James W. Underhill

Edinburgh University Press

© James W. Underhill, 2009, 2013

First published in hardback by Edinburgh University Press 2009

Edinburgh University Press Ltd
22 George Square, Edinburgh EH8 9LF

www.euppublishing.com

Typeset in Ehrhardt
by Servis Filmsetting Ltd, Stockport, Cheshire, and
printed and bound in Great Britain by
CPI Antony Rowe, Chippenham and Eastbourne

A CIP record for this book is available from the British Library

ISBN 978 0 7486 3842 0 (hardback)
ISBN 978 0 7486 6879 3 (paperback)

The right of James W. Underhill
to be identified as author of this work
has been asserted in accordance with
the Copyright, Designs and Patents Act 1988.

Contents

Acknowledgements

I would like to thank Cambridge University Press for kindly allowing me to reproduce quotations from Peter Heath's Translation of Wilhelm von Humboldt's *On Language: The Diversity of Human Language Structure and its Influence on the Mental Development of Mankind*, edited by Michael Losonsky (2nd edition published in 1999). Without these passages, this work would obviously have been impossible. I would also like to thank the same Press for allowing me to publish passages from John A. Lucy's *Language Diversity and Thought: A Reformulation of the Linguistic Relativity Hypothesis* (1992). Lucy's work allowed me to enrich the chapters on both Sapir and Whorf. I also wish to thank the MIT Press for allowing me to reproduce sections from Benjamin Lee Whorf's *Language, Thought and Reality*, edited by John B. Caroll (1984). For helping me with the arduous task of checking the manuscript, I wish to warmly thank both Marko Pajević (without whose aid, the analysis of German would have suffered), Vicki Briault Magnus, whose remarks and suggestions on style considerably improved the English, and François Genton. All these people gave me exactly the right kind of encouragement during that difficult period of seclusion and intense intellectual questioning which fills one full of doubts as to the nature and *raison d'être* of an academic project of this kind. For the same reason, I am grateful to one of the great contemporary Humboldt scholars, Jürgen Trabant of Berlin. His enthusiasm for this short book was inspiring and his criticisms have helped present Humboldt's ideas with greater accuracy. Thanks also to the editorial staff of Edinburgh University Press for their help and support.

Preface

The global era might be seen as the *era of language* or the *era of the threat to language*, depending on what we mean by language. If we survey the astounding advances made in the field of communication with the advent of portable telephones, email, video conferences and IT, then we might be tempted to celebrate our era for brushing aside barriers to communication throughout the world. But if we consider language, not as communication, but as that specific system that evolves over time to give expression to a people's culture, its way of life and even its way of thinking, then our era looks somewhat less rosy. Some experts estimate that of the 6,000 languages now spoken in the world, no more than half will survive the twenty-first century.

English seems assured a future. Is it conceivable for the average English-speaker, that the language which gave the world William Shakespeare, Isaac Newton and Adam Smith should simply cease to exist? This, nevertheless, is the fate facing thousands of languages whose communities are either dying out or switching over to languages which have greater clout in the world of international commerce, languages which are likely to provide their speakers with greater hope of economic survival. One language (the work of centuries of thought and feeling refined into expression) simply dies out every two weeks it has been estimated. A library of a culture is burned down often without ever having been written.

One of the great questions of the twenty-first century, not only for linguists and anthropologists, but for all those who feel concerned by the destiny of the human species as a culturally evolving project, will be the language question. If the human species can only evolve by virtue of individuals communicating in and with language, what should we do about the destruction of language systems which fall by the wayside while a minority of languages belonging to economically powerful and culturally dominant communities assert themselves more and more in the global world? In response to this question, it seems likely that two camps will oppose one another. One camp will extol the virtues of a world language (an English to replace the Latin of the Classical and Medieval eras), a language which allows different peoples throughout the world to find shared solutions to global problems such as war, ecological damage and the energy shortage. The other camp will lament the annihilation of different cultural perspectives and knowledge which might have been assimilated into the global culture if they had not been dismissed by bodies and institutions indifferent to diversity and blind to what other cultures and languages have to offer. Indeed, since the 1990s, the latter group has been mobilising its resources to raise consciousness as to the danger of language death.

Though this may be a crucial debate, this small book is intended as a defence of neither side. The aim set out here is far more modest: the objective is simply to clarify the terms with which this debate will be conducted. The essential terms around which our debate will revolve are *language, thought* and *worldview*. Though the first two seem fairly straightforward, it will become clear that very different meanings are being attached to them depending on who is speaking. The last word, *worldview*, is considerably more complicated. The term itself is attributed to Wilhelm von Humboldt (1767–1835), the German politician and philologist. It has been adopted by numerous linguists, however, and has become associated within specialist circles with what is known as the Sapir-Whorf hypothesis which posits that thought is language-dependant. In non-specialist circles, *worldview* has come to denote the perspective of a culture. Such a usage of the term can be found in the works of sociologists, historians and cultural thinkers just as it can also be found in the literature of international organisations such as UNESCO and political institutions such as the European Union.

And what has become of Wilhelm von Humboldt? Despite the success of his term, Humboldt himself has, to a large extent, been forgotten in the English-speaking world. Why should this be? Perhaps it is the difficulty of his writing that made Humboldt's claim to posterity precarious. Linguists like the American, Noam Chomsky (born 1928) and philosophers like the German Martin Heidegger (1889–1976) have praised the profundity of Humboldt's linguistic philosophy, but have often bewailed the density of his reflections. In answer to their complaints, I have tried here to present the English-speaker with a reasonably easy introduction to Humboldt's thought on language and worldview. This should achieve three aims.

Firstly, however interesting the English-speaking accounts of worldview may be, this book should demonstrate that the concept of worldview as Humboldt presented it has been severely curtailed and vulgarised in the models of the relationship between thought and language that are to be found in the works of English-speaking linguists. Secondly, it should allow us to enter the rich and dynamic model of language that Humboldt offers in his linguistic philoso-phy, a model in which the individual both shapes and is shaped by the *organ of speech*, a model in which language is considered to be the constantly developing, creative endeavour of a whole culture. Thirdly, by clarifying the terms of the debate concerning the rela-tionship between worldview and language, it should allow more refined formulations of arguments, whether they be in defence of global communication or of individual languages.

For the moment, one camp seems indifferent to language death and meets the lamentation of well-meaning ethnolinguists (and *ecolinguists*) with scepticism. This scepticism derives from the firmly held belief that all languages allow us to speak about the world in pretty much the same way. Foreign languages, in such a model, are simply different word lists in which the terms applied to things differ from our own terms. The logical conclusion that such a model leads us to is: Why not use English instead? Though this may be a very naïve view of language, it is one that has fuelled research into machine translation in recent years. And the success of translation in general goes some way to supporting the belief that ideas can in fact be transferred from very different cultures to our own. Ideas can, it would seem, reach from one worldview into another. Communication between worldviews, though problematic, *is* possible.

If ethnolinguists are to combat scepticism about linguistic diversity they will have to provide a very different, and much more rigorous model of language than the communicative model that has come to occupy a central place in the globalisation debate. To date, no such model exists. Well-intentioned defenders of linguistic diversity have tended to assume that each language is a worldview. Such an assumption is rarely backed up with any profound experience of the worldview in question. Indeed the very project to defend multiple languages makes it inevitable that the defenders themselves are likely to have little or no real knowledge of the language they are defending. Defending the worldview of dying communities becomes, therefore, an act of faith. Though the intuition that each language allows its speakers entry into a unique worldview may be perspicacious, it remains as yet unproven, and a serious debate on linguistic diversity can hardly be founded upon blind faith.

Humboldt, an empirically-minded child of the Enlightenment, proceeded in a much more lucid manner. In contrast to the enthusiastic politics of the defenders of diversity, he devoted his life to the painstaking study of linguistic differences in the hope of catching a glimpse of what made a language essentially and radically unique as a representation of the way individuals within a community formulated the world around them. If this book allows us entry into Humboldt's thought, and if his thought allows linguists to reformulate their ideas as to the relationship between language and worldview more rigorously, it will have achieved its aim.

Part I: Language and World

CHAPTER I

The Word is a World
(*La parole est un monde*)

Linguists by profession and by inclination are attracted to the multiple varieties of speech and language that have grown up in the world. Diversity has been celebrated and, now that languages appear to be dying out with increasing speed, many linguists (Crystal, Dalby, Nettle, Romaine, Hagège et al.) have taken it upon themselves to strive to save them while there is still time. In the discourse of such authors, languages are *endangered*, almost *extinct*. The French linguist, Claude Hagège (born in Tunisia in 1936) eloquently sings the praises of 'living languages' (*les langues vivantes*) in his book, *Put an End to the Death of Languages* (*Halte à la mort des langues*, 2002). For Hagège the diversity of languages is a symbol of life itself (2002: 33):

> Dans le monde du vivant, le foisonnement des espèces est une des images de la vie, qu'il s'agisse des insectes ou des graminées. La diversité des langues, surgissement torrentueux de la vie, est un motif d'émerveillement pour ceux qui n'ont pas peur de les apprendre, et aussi, on veut l'espérer, pour les linguistes eux-mêmes. (ibid.)

> In the living world, the burgeoning of species is one of life's images, whether we are thinking of insects or types of grass. The diversity of languages, this torrent-like surging forth of life, is something which strikes with wonder those who are

not afraid to learn languages and, we might hope, linguists themselves. (my translation, 'mT', hereafter)

Languages (the author asserts) are the havens in which we deposit our lives (2002: 19). Languages contain our history. And, Hagège argues, every philologist knows that we deposit in our languages those 'treasures which recount the development of societies and the adventures of individuals' (ibid.).

In a slightly less lyrical vein, the English-speaking linguist David Crystal (born in 1941 in Northern Ireland and brought up in Wales) takes up the defence of endangered languages, because for him a language represents 'a guide to understanding a community's world view' (*Language Death*, 2000: 49). Crystal claims it is time to promote the new ethnolinguistics, or what he and other like-minded linguists call *ecolinguistics*. Crystal adopts a staunchly pragmatic stance, advocating a series of measures for promoting endangered languages (or rather for 'revitalising' them). He even goes as far as advocating the establishment of a 'Revitalising Team' (2002: 154–63) which will serve to catalogue different aspects of the endangered language and strive to revalorise its status both inside and outside the endangered linguistic community.

Whenever linguists condemn language death, they are not simply lamenting the loss of a lexis different from their own, an alternative set of labels for things in the world around us. Neither are they thinking primarily of grammar. A few specialists may find different grammatical structures fascinating, but it is not grammar that is at the heart of the discussion of language death either. The great thrust behind this belated attempt to save disappearing languages comes from a premise, commonly held among linguists, according to which different languages represent different worldviews. According to the logic of this hypothesis, we construct conceptually the world around us by using our language. We begin to do this as soon as we begin to learn to speak: we listen to the people we hear speaking all around us, and thereby adopt the language which previous generations pass on to us as part of a continuous, ongoing and unbroken living tradition. This process continues as we learn to read and digest the culture of earlier épochs as it is distilled in the form of written texts. We understand the world in which we live with the resources of, and within the framework of, language if this hypothesis is well founded. The logical consequence of such a view is that losing a language entails losing a stance from which to view the world, i.e. losing knowledge and understanding. With the death of a language, a culture dies. So the argument goes.

If this is so, then the crusade to save languages is indeed urgent. And the enthusiasm of linguists can be seen as a direct reaction to the indifference of globalisation, a process which seems to be crushing linguistic communities out of existence. However, in the great wave of enthusiastic support for endangered languages, in the great crusade against their demise, there has often been a laxity in conceptual definition, and this must surely be eradicated if we are to conceive in clear terms the relationship between concepts and words, between languages and the world. English-speakers will also perhaps find it difficult to understand that this great project to save languages (which have all but been abandoned by the communities which once spoke them), has often been confused with (and indeed at times animated by) a rejection of American culture and the English language along with that culture. In an ill-defined antipathy for the US and the global economy (with which it is often assimilated) linguists have sometimes (and non-specialists have often) assumed that it is the growing predominance of English which has brought about the precarious status of little-spoken languages. A mistrust of major languages is not absent throughout the work of the French linguist, Hagège. And a similar mistrust is characteristic of journalism in France in which a defence of the French language in the face of the new Big Brother, English, has led to a curious feeling of sympathy for, and solidarity with, endangered languages. Anti-English sentiment has inspired attempts to promote what might be called *resentful fraternities*, attempts by members of less prolific languages to find once more the common roots that their language shares with other languages and to promote their shared traditions. Rapprochements between Romance languages are only one example. In the French case, it seems clear that concern that English is gaining ground has made some linguists fearful that the fate of languages dying today might be the fate of their own language in a century or two to come.

This climate of suspicion and resentment is difficult for British or American citizens to understand. For the English-speaker, it will seem surprising that French linguists sometimes feel a certain empathy for the fate of dying and disappearing languages. How can there can be any comparison made between Polabian (whose demise Hagège regrets, 2002: 81) and French? Polabian was a Slavic language which disappeared in the eighteenth century. French is a prolific world language which was more widely spoken than English at the time of Polabian's disappearance, and French remains today one of the main languages of many African countries and an important language within the European Union.

Nevertheless, the cultural climate in France and many other countries is one of a defiant defence of diversity. Diversity is being celebrated and promoted as an antidote to the encroaching hegemony of the Anglo-American culture and language. In the defence of alternative worldviews and endangered languages, there is a latent but implicit attack on English as a framework within which to understand the world.

It is within such a context, then, that we should view the publication of Anne Stamm's *The Word is a World* (*La parole est un monde*) published in France in 1999. Stamm has written what might in many ways be considered a short and pleasant introduction to African culture. It is an anthropological account rather than a linguistic one, and Stamm in no way claims that she intends to further what has become known as *linguistic anthropology* as contemporary American scholars such as Salzmann or Lucy might define it. She intends to provide, for a largely non-specialist audience in France, an explanation of African culture as a whole. Consequently, she explains the importance of proverbs, songs, dances and rituals for handing down *sagesse* (the wisdom of the elders): wisdom which fashions the way people live, the relations between generations, between sexes, and the relationship of men and women to work, to war, to family and ultimately to their god, gods or demigods.

Throughout this investigation, Stamm insists upon the importance of speech. The various cultures she deals with are oral cultures, cultures within which the voice takes on a theatrical and moral role in imposing tradition and handing that tradition on to the next generation. It will not escape French readers that Stamm uses the word *parole* to designate this key concept: *la parole* is often used as the word of God, *The Word*. While an English Christian spreads *the good word*, a French Christian *prêche la bonne parole*.

Early on in her short work, Stamm establishes the link between speech and spirituality. For the Dogons of Mali, there are, Stamm claims (26), several versions of creation, but Stamm selects the one in which speech is of paramount importance. In this version, God is both thinker and speaker (*penseur et parleur*). The essence of creation (*Amma*, in the Dogons' language) is *parole*, and the essence of *parole* is communication, Stamm affirms, quoting the translation of a proverb quoted by D. Zahan. God speaks creation into existence (25).

A language is not only a worldview then: language brings the world into being. Our Judeo-Christian culture offers a similar account and, therefore, makes such a claim both comprehensible and familiar. Stamm is clearly attributing to *parole* not only the physical character it possesses as understood as *everyday speech*: she is opening up the term to a metaphysical dimension. Though the Greek term *logos*, which we translate into *the Word*, in The Gospel according to St John ('In the Beginning was *the Word*'), is usually translated into French as *le Verbe*, it is clear that Stamm is replacing this key term with *parole*. It is by remarrying the physical and the metaphysical, by linking everyday existence with the transcendental sphere, that she hopes to open up the exotic worldview of African languages to us.

Given the importance of speech for oral cultures, it is not surprising that Stamm devotes a chapter to *parole*, a chapter in which she considers the education of speech, the mastering of the voice and of good and bad speech ('La bonne et la mauvaise parole', 1999: 130). But in the closing section of the book, Stamm arrives at her ultimate goal: 'Toute chose est parole' (Everything is speech). She quotes Sory Camara who, in his *Paroles très anciennes* (Very Ancient Sayings), provides the line which gives Stamm her title: *La parole est un monde*. In this celebration of speech, Stamm claims that dance is a mode of communicating (140), rhythms speak to us (141), instruments have voices, each flute has his mouth (ibid.). Stamm concludes by considering the silent speech of statues which is extolled as being mute but efficient in that it offers protection to the group (144).

Sculptures, we are told, directly evoke concepts (Stamm 1999: 141). This is somewhat at odds with Stamm's central claim that African wisdom is not transmitted through concepts but through allegories, myths and dances (7). Other criticisms might also be levelled at Stamm, if we take up the investigation of the African worldview which she promises to reveal to us:

1. If a culture is contained within its language, can we rely on translations to allow us to enter into the worldview of that culture?
2. When considering the significance of the rhythm of proverbs and songs, are written accounts in French sufficient material for analysis? Stamm claims that the rhythm of the original can still be felt (10), but anyone who has ever tried to translate a French alexandrine (a twelve-syllable line of verse) into an English pentameter may have some doubts as to the survival of African speech rhythms in translation.
3. Are secondary sources published by European academics a reliable source of information about oral cultures?
4. Can all inherited culture or tradition be considered as wisdom?
5. Can we speak of the worldview of a continent? A worldview is usually associated with a single language, and indeed to speak of a language's worldview is to stress the individual nature of that language. Stamm lumps all African languages together, and it remains unclear whether she speaks any of them.
6. If everything is speech, and speech is everything, how are we supposed to discuss the relationship between speech and other things, thought, culture, and the individual, for instance?

Stamm offers a colourful little book in which she does not pretend to resolve the question of the relationship between language and thought. Like the books of proverbs from our own culture and like dictionaries of expressions from foreign languages, readers might find her book stimulating and amusing. However, if we are to consider the question of worldviews and evaluate the loss to the world of the loss of a language, then we shall have to investigate our field of study with far greater conceptual rigour. True, Stamm, does not set herself up as a linguist, but her unquestioned conviction that each language engenders a rich and exotic world finds an echo in much contemporary celebration of linguistic diversity among linguists. However well-intentioned the supporters of *ecolinguistics* are, we should be uncompromising when it comes to criticising any conceptual laxity in their thought. And a healthy dose of scepticism might serve us well when we appraise the claims made by linguists about the richness of languages which defenders are unable to study without the aid of translators and translations. We can only speak of what we know, and as the example of Stamm shows, when we have no direct knowledge we would do best to proceed cautiously in our affirmations.

Stamm offers us an exotic tour of a continent of languages. But can we trust our guide? Does she not seek to seduce us with her own longings and imaginings? She offers us the voice of spiritual Africa singing to us. But is this not the echo of a spiritual bankruptcy in the West seeking solace elsewhere? In a word, we cannot know. Only by painstaking work and long years of practice can we acquire sufficient knowledge of a language to begin tracing the outlines of its worldview and comparing it with our own.

Each language may be a world in the sense that it contains a distinct conception of the world, but there are no means of verifying this hypothesis. To do so would entail knowing every language as a native speaker knows his own. For this reason we would do well to proceed tentatively. And we should take care to avoid the trap Stamm lays for herself in celebrating one aspect of language and culture (*la parole*) by filling it with a multitude of concepts which risk rendering it ambiguous and obscure. Only once we have clearly defined the term *worldview* can we hope to appraise with any analytical rigour the hypothesis that the way we experience the world is in some way related to the way we speak of it. And we cannot simply assume that thought and language are related, because to do so would be to assume that the terms themselves (thought and language) are straightforward. In the following chapters it will become clear that the situation is somewhat more complicated.

CHAPTER 2

What Do We Have in Mind When We Talk about Language?

'The case of language,' Noam Chomsky posited in *Language and Mind* (1972: ix), 'is particularly interesting because language plays an essential role in thinking [. . .].' David Crystal, in The *Cambridge Encyclopaedia of Language* (1997), does not seem to contest this point: 'It seems evident that there is the closest of relationships between language and thought: everyday experience suggests that much of our thinking is facilitated by language' (14).

Crystal goes on to ask an essential question: 'But is there identity between the two? Is it possible to think without language? Or does our language dictate the ways in which we are able to think?' In *Language, Ideology and Point of View* (1993), Paul Simpson adopts the line that language does in fact direct our thinking. Because viewpoints become both consciously and unconsciously *encoded*, we are influenced into either going along with them or rejecting them. For Simpson, language is anything but a transparent, objective medium of communication: it is a 'projection of positions and perspectives . . . a way of communicating attitudes and assumptions' (quoted by Thomas et al. 2004: 32).

There would seem to be some degree of agreement among linguists belonging to diverse schools that thought and language are closely bound up together. If this hypothesis is well founded then it would certainly seem to back up the argument of Stamm and ecolinguists like Hagège and Crystal that a people's worldview is inseparable from the language it speaks. Whether our conception of the world is reflected in language, or whether it is language itself which enables us to frame the concepts with which we communicate remains a controversial question, but the idea that the two are interrelated has gained general acceptance among many scholars.

However, if we are to consider the relationship between the two, we can hardly accept the terms themselves without first defining them. What do we mean by thought? What do we have in mind when we think about thinking? If language helps give form to thought, does that imply that language is essential to memory, to contemplation, to feeling? And if feeling is not held to be thinking, how should we distinguish between the two? Poets, such as T. S. Eliot, have objected to the distinction, as if to contend that rationalist thinking has tended to obscure other equally fundamental forms of thinking and expression (forms which poets have continued to cultivate). Traditionally, these latter forms of thinking and expression have been attributed to imagination and the freedom of the individual's creative intelligence. But if we accept them as forms of thinking, doesn't the very idea of a free and creative form of thinking preclude a deterministic model in which language channels or directs thought?

Crystal, in his encyclopaedia entry (1997: 15), rejects the deterministic model of the relationship between language and thought, a model which would make the speaking subject an automaton which acts out the orders of an all-controlling language, a model in which language itself is conceived as animated and personified while the individual is inversely objectified and *depersonalised*. But Crystal claims that language can, nevertheless, 'influence the way we perceive and remember, and it affects the way we perform mental tasks.' For Crystal, the types of mental acts that involve language are forms which involve 'reasoned thinking which takes place as we work out problems, tell stories, plan strategies, and so on. It has been called "rational", "directed", "logical", or "propositional" thinking' (14).

If this has gone some way to refining our idea of *thought*, we still have to ask ourselves what we mean by *language*. This may seem an absurd and pedantic question, until we try to translate the word: then it becomes clear that several concepts inhabit this single word. Modern French distinguishes between *langue* and *langage*.

Langue is usually reserved for the language system which is made up of words, phrases, texts and grammatical rules pertaining to a given linguistic community (the French people for example, or the Portuguese). *Langage* has two definitions: it designates firstly, the faculty of speech, and secondly, the specific linguistic qualities and attributes of an individual text or speech act. While an Englishman has this latter definition in mind when he praises the 'language of Shakespeare', the French often have in mind the English language as a system when they speak of *la langue de Shakespeare*.

Like English, German, it is true, has only one word for language, *Sprache*, but it would be a mistake to assimilate words and concepts and to imagine that German speakers are incapable of maintaining the same conceptual distinctions as those the French have at their disposal. Besides, German makes a distinction between *Sprache* and *Rede*. While the former refers to both the capacity for speaking and to the linguistic system of their linguistic community, *Rede* can be easily translated into English using the term *speech*. The French translator, on the other hand, when faced with *Rede* or *speech*, will be forced to choose between *parole* (which may mean *word* or *words*, the *act of speaking* and can even mean a *promise*) and *discours* (which we might translate as *a speech*, in the public or political sense of the term, or a *style of speaking*, as in, for example, the style of speaking characteristic of Tony Blair and New Labour).

One of the almost insurmountable difficulties involved in learning a foreign language is that we inevitably try to translate foreign words back into the concepts of our native language. We are almost incapable of shedding the naïve belief that bilingual dictionaries can provide us with a series of wholly reliable conceptual equations. The truth of the matter is far more complex. Words like *language* take on different meanings in different contexts. And the complexity of our concept of language which is so clearly illustrated by the problem of translating the word should alert us to the fact that those who agree that thought and language are related, often have very different concepts of thought and language in mind. To put it in other terms, their agreement is founded on shifting sands.

Some clarification seems necessary. When Chomsky contends that below the apparent manifest differences between languages, there exists a *universal grammar*, he is referring to a very different concept of language than Simpson when he speaks of language directing our thought. Simpson is concerned with the style of language adopted in the popular press, the rhetoric of what might be called *propaganda*. He is referring to one type of discourse within the English language as a cultural system. Chomsky, on the other hand, is speaking about the differences between different systems (e.g. between German and English).

Clearly, if we contend that language and thought are linked (or indeed inextricable) we must first prevent ourselves from confusing the terms we are linking. It is one thing to say that the German worldview is different from the French one (a common enough contention that first came into vogue at the end of the eighteenth century when the Marquise de Staël made conversation about the distinction between the two languages a fashionable party game for the erudite intellectuals of her salons). It is another thing to suggest that Blair's worldview is not one that is acceptable to traditional Labour Party members. The first hypothesis posits an essential difference in the language system with which or within which a people thinks; the second, that radically different ideologies and individual perspectives can be formulated in speech within the same language system. How have these two very different ideas come to be confused in the term *worldview*? And where does this term come from?

CHAPTER 3

What Do We See in the Term Worldview?

Worldview is a term with a colourful past. For many French scholars, it has an American origin and is associated primarily with what has come to be known as the *Whorf-Sapir hypothesis*, according to which 'a language's difference results in a different intellectual and affective structuring' for the mind of the speaker of a language community (Dubois et al. 1994: 511, mT). The term has been traced back from its use by Benjamin Lee Whorf (1897–1941) and his teacher, Edward Sapir (1884–1939), to the work of the great anthropologist, Franz Boas (1858–1942), who is responsible for having stressed the importance of language for culture in his ethnological exploration of Amerindian cultures. Indeed, it was the confrontation with the very different cultures and languages of North America that forced linguists (used to working within the frameworks of Indo-European languages) to re-evaluate some of their fundamental premises about language. In this sense, the origin of the term is, indirectly, more Amerindian than American. It is also worth noting that both Boas and Sapir were of Jewish-German origin, Boas having emigrated to the United States in his late twenties and Sapir having been brought there as a child of five years old. Both no doubt drew on their knowledge of Hebrew and German as alternative worldviews to the outlook American English offered as the natural ordering of the world. Whorf, in contrast to these two, moves into foreign languages more as a crusader moves into the unknown, and there is a latent radicalism in his thought which surfaces at times to give a dogmatic turn to the way he expresses the differences in nature between languages. For Boas and Sapir, in contrast, linguistic diversity was a fact of everyday life. In his defence of Amerindian languages, Whorf is a defender of the underdogs. There was a benevolent concern for alternative cultures in his work which is, in emotional terms, more akin to contemporary ecolinguistics than the sober philology of Sapir or the anthropology of Boas with its positivist scientific methodology.

The radicalism of Whorf has had unfortunate consequences for the reception of the term *worldview* and for debate concerning the work of Sapir and Whorf, and what has come to be called *mentalist linguistics* (Malmkjaer 1991: 303–8). The concentration on Whorf's more radical writings – often the reduction of them to a few standard quotes (Crystal 1997: 15, Dubois et al. 1994: 511, Auroux 1996: 167–71) has tended to obscure both the question of the relation between language and the mind as well as the origin of the term *worldview*. The German origin is attested to by the use of the German term *Weltanschauung* by Whorf himself in *Language, Thought and Reality* ([1956] 1984: 58) and many scholars (Crystal, Salzmann et al.) have quoted Wilhelm von Humboldt as the author who coined the term.

Nonetheless, Humboldt's work is rarely quoted and the discussion of the relationship between mind and worldview invariably shifts to a brief consideration of Whorf's radical relativism which is, in turn, either embraced or rejected in whole or in part. The contemporary American Christian thinker David K. Naugle, in his fascinating book-length exploration of the term *worldview* (*Worldview: The History of a Concept*: 2002), traces the origin of the term *Weltanschauung* to Kant (59–60). He does mention Humboldt's use of the term, but only fleetingly, and the fact that he refers to him as 'Alexander von Humboldt's brother' indicates the weight Naugle accords to him in his study. (Indeed the philologist is quoted only by referring to one secondary source.)

Naugle's treatment of Humboldt is characteristic of the failure of the English-speaking culture to understand and adopt the thought of this prolific philosopher of language. Indeed, we have never grasped to any satisfactory degree the concept of worldview, as it was linguistically extrapolated in the thought of Humboldt;

i.e. worldview as the fundamental and necessary processing of the world by the mind through the faculty of language. This was the human capacity which intrigued Humboldt, and it was by painstakingly examining the different ways in which each language assimilates the world and organises its concepts for what *is* and what *takes place* within the world, that Humboldt hoped to make worldview a primary conceptual tool for understanding and classifying languages. Despite often being quoted by modern linguists, however, Humboldt's great twofold project to compare the languages of the world and the worlds that they permit us to enter into has come to all but nothing as Humboldt scholars such as Trabant (1992) and translators of his works such as Thouard (in Humboldt 2000) have pointed out.

This becomes all too clear when we consider that Humboldt's fundamental concept of worldview, the subject of this short work, has been lost in French and English (as it has to a large extent in German). For Humboldt's contribution to the worldview debate was to develop the concept of *Weltansicht*, not the concept of *Weltanschauung* which has managed to take root in certain debates in English and which became rather more widespread in French in the twentieth century. Since Humboldt's term is rarely quoted in German and since, when Humboldt's thought is spoken of in German-speaking circles, his concept of worldview is often misunderstood in terms of the more widely used term *Weltanschauung*, it is hardly surprising that the distinction between the two terms has not gained currency in English-speaking linguistics. Indeed it was not until recent decades that the German philologist, Jürgen Trabant (born in 1942), one of the leading Humboldt scholars, proposed a clear distinction between the two terms.

Weltanschauung has been attributed a wide variety of meanings, but has often been used to refer to a personal stance, a view of the world which is more deeply intuitive than a philosophy. For this reason, it was attractive for the Romantics, offering them an alternative to the all-embracing concept of Reason heralded by the Enlightenment. In the twentieth century, it tended to be associated less with individuals than with social groups. Consequently, political movements often adopted the term, often using it as a synonym for ideology (Naugle 2002). As Trabant makes clear in his crucial distinction (1992), *Weltansicht* refers to the way the language system shapes the perspective and conception we have of the world and to a large extent shapes the way we negotiate our way through the course of life on a day-to-day basis as we converse with others. Though the forces which shape our perception and conception of the world do not often rise to the level of consciousness (since language is the telescope and not the object we use it to focus upon), we tend to take the instrument we use for granted. This does not mean, however, that the individual man cannot reflect upon his *Weltansicht*. On the contrary, this was Humboldt's very project as a thinker and linguist. Nor did it mean that the individual man could not act upon his *Weltansicht*. On the contrary, Humboldt argued that consciously or unconsciously we all constantly act upon our shared *Weltansicht* as we re-enact patterns of thought in language or break out into original forms of expression. For this reason, Humboldt's study of language took on an inseparable double objective; to consider the way the language system shapes the thought of a culture, and to consider the contribution made to the development of that culture by exceptional individuals who were capable of invigorating the vibrant living impulse of speech as a mode for conception and expression.

Trabant's distinction which is bolstered by Anne-Marie Chabrolle-Cerretini (2007: 59–81) helps to highlight the vital impulse of the Humboldt project and disentangle it from the concept of *Weltanschauung* as it might be understood by philosophers, sociologists and poets. It remains to be seen whether Humboldt's mature concept of *Weltansicht* can be transposed into contemporary linguistics in the English-speaking world. If it can be, it is likely to cause a small earthquake, because Humboldt's conception of language, culture, man and worldview forces us to question many of the concepts we take for granted and reintroduces to language-study questions of thought and culture which have tended in the last two centuries to be left to philosophers and anthropologists. Certainly, the present work aims to reconsider the terms of the worldview debate in the light of Humboldt's project, and this in turn will necessitate a complete overhaul of the taxonomy used in that debate. But first let's consider in further detail the origin of the term *worldview* in French and English and the way it became entangled with *Weltanschauung*.

Thouard, a contemporary French translator of Humboldt, adopts Trabant's distinction and regrets that both terms have been assimilated into one concept in French, usually referred to as *vision du monde* (Humboldt 2000: 180–2). Thouard claims that *Weltansicht* in Humboldt's work is used to designate the concept according to which 'each speaker of a language is led by its structure and by the particular modes in which meaning is put into form in that language, to divide his experience in a certain manner' (181, mT). *Weltanschauung*, is not therefore a synonym of *Weltansicht* (as Naugle claims, 2000: 7). *Weltanschauung*, as a term, has a far greater scope of meaning and has been used to mean *ideology*, or *belief system* in German, French and English. *Weltanschauung* does appear in Humboldt's work (Humboldt 1999: 140) when he talks of 'the living *sensory world-outlook*' in Peter Heath's translation of 'der lebendigen, sinnlichen Weltanschauung' (*Über die Verschiedenheit des menschlichen Sprachbaues*, 2003: 403). But Thouard argues (in Humboldt 2000:182), that in Humboldt's thought *Weltanschauung* is sufficiently clearly defined as meaning man's intimate need to produce language in order to develop his intellectual forces and to realise a conception of the world, a process which requires the clarification of his own thoughts in his speech with others. *Weltansicht* operates at a far more fundamental level and refers to man's first contact with the reality of the world, a visual or sensory contact. *Weltansicht* therefore precedes the forming of a *Weltanschauung* which can include various beliefs. *Weltansicht* does not interpret the world: it enables man to form a concept of the world 'by furnishing him with a prior linguistic comprehension of the world' (Thouard, ibid., mT). When Thouard argues that the two concepts have been confused in one catch-all concept in French (182), he is describing the same course of conceptual development that is found in the worldview debate in English.

It would seem then that the concept of *worldview* is far from straightforward. As in English circles, we will find much consensus among French linguists that language and worldview (*la langue* and *la vision du monde*) are linked. Czech scholars have also adopted the concept of worldview, though they have accentuated the visual aspect latent in the term, rendering it as *obraz světa* (Vaňková 2001) which might be translated back into English as *world image* or *picture of the world*. Czech scholars are investigating the relationship between language and worldview using this term. But the Czechs like the French and the English have lost sight of the original impetus which inspired Humboldt to carve the concept of *Weltansicht* as distinct from *Weltanschauung* by distinguishing between (1) the way language opens up to us a network of concepts with which to understand and interpret the world and communicate our thoughts and feelings about it, and (2) the way this capacity which is given to us by language allows us to go on to formulate different concepts and belief systems concerning the world in which we live.

Though Langham Brown's excellent work, *Wilhelm von Humboldt's Conception of Linguistic Relativity* (1967), goes some way to uncovering Humboldt's project, few scholars have quoted Humboldt at any length in their discussion of the relationship between language and thought. One noteworthy exception is the English scholar and specialist of translation, George Steiner (1975), who stresses the importance of *Weltansicht* for language and, consequently, for translation (which becomes, if we adopt Humboldt's perspective) a voyage between different worldviews. It remains unclear though whether Steiner's writings have encouraged English-speaking linguists to return to the study of Humboldt's writings.

Some philological archaeology would therefore seem to be in order. But before proceeding to discuss Humboldt's project in further detail, justice must be done to the American tradition, since even a cursory study like the one which follows will reveal a far richer account than the one encapsulated in *The Sapir-Whorf Hypothesis* as it has come to be understood. It is worth considering what has become of *worldview* in the American tradition reaching from Boas to Whorf to contemporary scholars of anthropological linguistics such as Malotki, Lee, Lucy and Salzmann. Once this has been done, we will be able to see more clearly what has been lost in the discussion of the relationship between thought and language with the loss of Humboldt and to what extent his thought might allow us to reformulate the terms of our discussion.

CHAPTER 4

Boas

It is difficult for us to appreciate today the importance of Franz Boas' *Handbook of American Indian Languages*, with its groundbreaking introduction in which he made a serious philological effort to present the complexities and subtleties of Amerindian languages to an audience which was inclined to believe that the thought, culture and language of these diverse peoples reflected a primitive state of evolution. Boas wrote his *Handbook* back in 1911, more than twenty years before the Nazis attempted to exterminate what they felt to be a race of *Untermenschen*. And he was writing in opposition to what was considered to be a perfectly respectable linguistic tradition incarnated by August Schleicher, the nineteenth-century philologist (1821–1868) who pushed the organic representation of language to an extreme form when he claimed that while some languages were advanced, there were, in contrast, primitive forms, such as those found in North America, which were wholly 'inapt for historical life' because of the excessive abundance of their forms (Hagège 2000: 28). According to Schleicher, such languages were destined to go into regression and would finally become extinct. To Schleicher this was only natural: primitive languages, as a like-minded linguist, Hovelacque, argued (Hagège 2000: 34, mT) 'perished in the pitiful struggle for survival.' Linguists of the time were eager to adopt the organic determinism of Social Darwinism and formulated ideas on the development of language and linguistic change within the prism of evolutionary theory. And it was within the context of this fashionable reformulation of the nature of language that Boas took his radical stance.

The main thrust of Boas' investigations aimed to discredit the coupling of race and language. Boas introduced a tripartite model in which he posited that:

[. . .] anatomical type, language, and culture have not necessarily the same fates; [. . .] a people may remain constant in type and language and change in culture; [. . .] they may remain constant in type, but change in language; or [. . .] they may remain constant in language and change in type and culture. (1973: 7)

While Boas stressed the importance of the relationship between culture and language, he rejected the hypothesis that language dictates culture:

It does not seem likely [. . .] that there is any direct relationship between the culture of the tribe and the language they speak, except in so far as the form of the language will be moulded by the state of culture, but not in so far as a certain state of culture is conditioned by morphological traits of the language. (1973: 63)

It is interesting to note, however, that Boas was convinced that all languages divide experience into conceptual classifications and that these classifications differ from language to language. He quotes the division into different sexes or genders as one case in point (ibid.). And he went on to state:

The behaviour of primitive man makes it perfectly clear that all these concepts, though they are in constant use, have never risen into consciousness, and that consequently their origin must be sought, not in rational, but in entirely unconscious, we may perhaps say instinctive, processes of the mind. (ibid.)

This seems to support the hypothesis that languages have a deep influence on thought, behaviour and culture, but as one contemporary commentator, the American linguist, John A. Lucy, explains: 'In the end, it seems that Boas's two desires, to assert the psychic unity of man and to avoid premature generalization at the theoretical level, kept him from going further along this line of thought . . .' (Lucy 1996: 16). This curious hesitancy probably reflects Boas' desire to avoid the commonly practised interpretation of differences in languages as proof of the richness of one or the poverty of another. True, he argues that Amerindian languages do not seem to have developed abstract terms in the way Indo-European languages have. When speaking of sight, Boas argues, Indians will point to an eye which sees, rather than having recourse to the abstract idea of an 'organ' or 'an instrument for seeing'. Native American languages (at least at the time Boas studied them) seemed to have no words for *essence* and *existence*. But Boas (in dismissing Western philosophy) seems to have been essentially a cultural relativist, because he argues that this proves only that these languages saw no need for the abstractions which our philosophical traditions have passed down to us (1973: 60).

Boas concentrated upon the modes of classification in language and took pains to explain that in some languages several actions were seen to be grouped together as part of one generic function, while they would be perceived as very different kinds of action in another language. For example, in the Dakota language:

> The terms *naxta'ka* TO KICK, *paxta'ka* TO BIND IN BUNDLES, *yaxta'ka* TO BITE, *ic'a'xtaka*, TO BE NEAR TO, *boxta'ka* TO POUND, are all derived from the common element *xtaka* TO GRIP, which holds them together, while we use distinct words for expressing the various ideas. (1973: 22)

But in contrasting these different classifications, Boas seems to wish to demonstrate the absurdity of claims that one language is richer than another. Because, while the example above might be used to demonstrate the complexity of English in comparison to the Dakota language, the fact that words for different kinds of snow (falling snow, drifting snow and snowdrift) are derived from different roots, in his famous example of the language of the Eskimos (21–2), could be used to draw the inverse conclusion in comparing English with Amerindian languages.

If one language seems to lack a category which is thought to be essential to our language, this shows merely a difference in kind rather than in quality. While any sentence in English entails a temporal aspect manifested in the tense used, the Eskimo language finds a sentence which might be translated as *single man sick* is sufficient for *The man is sick*. This might seem strange to us of course, but the context in which the Eskimo phrase is spoken allows speakers to avoid confusion without specifying grammatically that we are talking about one specific man in the here and now. A similar example taken from an Indo-European language will perhaps help to demonstrate this more clearly. Russians find little use for their equivalent of our verb *to be* in many instances, so a Russian will find himself in no way hindered in using verbless phrases such as *Ja Ivan* (I Ivan) for introducing himself. If he *is* Ivan today, we would presume he was yesterday and will be tomorrow. The present tense is therefore redundant in this context. It is grammatical convention and not meaning that requires the verb in our English sentence. Besides, it should be remembered that our present simple tense is used most often to describe either states or repeated actions rather than anything that is going on at the present moment: *I swim* is never used when we find ourselves doing the breaststroke or the crawl, for example.

Boas was convinced that despite the differences in conceptual categories and in grammar, 'the most fundamental grammatical concepts in all languages must be considered as proof of the unity of fundamental psychological processes' (1973: 67). For Lucy:

> This view flows quite naturally from Boas's general argument that individual performance and ability are much the same in every culture, but that individuals are enmeshed in different traditions. (1996: 14)

But it is the differences between these traditions that Lucy highlights in his account of Boas' work, and in doing so, he seems to suggest that the anthropologist is grappling with a contradiction: as we look more closely at the conceptual frameworks that are implicit in speech, it becomes increasingly difficult to maintain that language does not influence culture. Boas himself seems to admit as much in the following two passages quoted by Lucy:

> [. . .] the categories of language compel us to see the world arranged in certain definite conceptual groups which, on account of our lack of knowledge of linguistic processes, are taken as objective categories and which, therefore, impose themselves upon the form of our thoughts. (Boas 1973, in Lucy 1996: 15)

> The form of our grammar compels us to select a few traits of thought we wish to express and suppresses many other aspects which the speaker has in mind and which the hearer supplies according to his fancy [. . .] There is little doubt that thought is thus directed in various channels . . . Such a tendency pervading the language may well lead to a different reaction to the incidents of everyday life and it is conceivable that in this sense the mental activities of a people may be in part directed by language. I should not be inclined to overestimate this influence because devices for expressing . . . [various ideas] are ever-present, and may rise in idiomatic use. In this sense, we may say that language exerts a limited influence on culture. (Boas in ibid.)

What starts as a rejection of determinism in the tripartite relationship between race, culture and language ends in a tentative hypothesis that language does indeed do more than simply reflect culture.

CHAPTER 5

Sapir

It is truly surprising that a thinker of such versatility as Edward Sapir (1882–1939) should come to be reduced to the minor partner in the *Sapir-Whorf hypothesis*. Sapir does have his defenders, but these tend to be specialists of his own work and, on the whole, little place has been found in contemporary linguistics for Sapir's theory of personality, for example, a theory in which he strove to define the patterns and forms common to both the psychological functioning of the individual and to culture as a whole. Sapir's mind was finely tuned to the examination of details and he never lost sight of the role played by the part within the whole of the language system. This is probably what helped Sapir recognise that the individual should always be maintained at the centre of any discussion of social interaction. Though he did perceive clearly the importance and the convenience of talking of groups and society as a whole when investigating psychological functioning, he was careful to remind us that the representations we construct of those pluralities are always derived from the model of the individual. To speak of how a community thinks or feels is misleading: though it can allow us to formulate meaningful descriptions and to distinguish between different societies, ultimately such sweeping statements cut us off from the study of actual living, breathing, interacting, speaking men and women. For Sapir, to speak of the unconscious of a society was no more than a personification since, as he wittily declared, 'society has no more of an unconscious than it has hands or legs' (Sapir 1985: 545).

Sapir's theory of the voice reflects this mode of thought. He analysed the specific properties of languages in terms of accentuation and intonation, and analysed individual voices in parallel in order to determine the ways a language constrains the voice and to what extent the individual voice expresses its own personality and its feeling within the scope of those constraints. Sapir's concern for the individual does not eclipse the project to compare languages, but the human voice as it manifests itself in the act of speaking, the individual addressing an individual in a given situation, was always central to Sapir's approach when he was comparing languages. Indeed, this attention to the personal expression of speech found its greatest expression in Sapir's own creative writing, because Sapir was also a poet.

The scientific aspirations of twentieth-century linguistics have tended to overshadow philology, which can be defined as the combined study of language, literature and culture. Consequently, in the decades following his death, little place has been found for Sapir's concerns for poetry or for the voice. Linguists are not often poets, and the very idea of writing poetry appears to some linguists a quaint but almost irrelevant pastime for those seriously concerned with language, a sidetrack to the highway of linguistics, with its scientific destination. But it is probably the fact that poets rework language and explore the boundaries of usage, reinventing expressions and pushing against the limits of common usage, that attracted Sapir to poetry, and in this he was the inheritor of Humboldt for whom poetry was central to the development of both language and the thought of the nation just as it formed part of the cultivation of the individual mind.

Sapir's contribution has been largely pushed to one side, however, and the leftovers of his investigations (what linguists of his time were able to understand and appreciate) have been summed up most often in the following quote in which the study of language is recommended to those of other disciplines because:

> Language is a guide to 'social reality.' Human beings do not live in the objective world alone, nor alone in the world of social activity as ordinarily understood, but are very much at the mercy of the particular language which has become the

medium of expression for their society. It is quite an illusion imagine that one adjusts to reality essentially without the use of language and that language is merely an incidental means of solving specific problems of communication or reflection. The fact of the matter is that the 'real world' is to a large extent unconsciously built up on the language habits of the group. No two languages are ever sufficiently similar to be considered as representing the same social reality. The worlds in which different societies live are distinct worlds, not merely the same world with different labels attached. (Sapir 1985: 162)

It is easy to see how this quote would be selected and celebrated by those anxious to defend the idea that a language represents a worldview. Sapir is clearly affirming here that it is only through the framework of language that man comes to form an idea of what he considers to be the 'real world'. Certainly, Sapir inherited from Boas the idea that languages were made up of different forms of conceptual categories. But, as Lucy points out: '. . . he added to Boas's views regarding the differences among the categories of various languages the notion that these categories are *arranged* into formally complete yet incommensurate systems' (1996: 17). What does Lucy have in mind when he speaks of 'incommensurate systems'? Languages elaborate patterns of thought. These patterns differ from language to language in the way they enable the mind to pose and resolve problems of expression. But each pattern forms part of a whole system which is endowed with an internal coherence. Each language is formally complete as a system and each language's internal coherence is unique. In Sapir's terms: ' [. . .] we may say that a language is so constructed that no matter what any speaker of it may desire to communicate . . . the language is prepared to do his work . . .' (Sapir in 1996: 17). This 'work' must vary from language to language since languages vary widely in their systematisation of fundamental concepts and the arrangement of their categories. As a result, languages are not directly translatable but only loosely equivalent to each other as symbolic devices.

As soon as we move beyond the level of the noun and the categorisation of individual things, as soon as we enter into the most simple sentence, any language tends to offer us moulds within which we think and speak, constructing our phrase from a multiplicity of implicit concepts which come to us intuitively. Such moulds appear to us to be so *natural* that we feel it would be pointless and laborious to analyse them. But this is precisely what Sapir invites us to do: to analyse the implicit concepts with which we speak. In one lengthy analysis in his book, *Language*, published in 1921, Sapir offers us the sentence, *the farmer kills the duckling*. As he says: 'We can visualize the farmer and the duckling and have also no difficulty in constructing an image of the killing' (Sapir 1949: 82–3). Without thinking, we make automatic use of the fact that the man involved in the killing is situated in relation to his profession *farming* which in turn situates him in his profession on *the farm*. In the same way *duckling* defines the duck in terms of size and age in relation to the adult duck using the diminutive form. The verb *to kill*, for us, is conceptually straightforward. This is not the case though in the German equivalent *tötet* in *Der Bauer tötet das Entlein*. Because German, unlike English, 'splits up the idea into the basic concept of "dead" (tot) and the derivational one of "causing to do (or be) so and so"' by changing the vowel and adding the suffix *–et* (1949: 91). Sapir goes on to point out that these aspects of meaning appear to form themselves immediately in our minds. In other languages, different implicit meanings will emerge just as effortlessly. The Kwakiutl Indian, for instance, would already have made an implicit choice, to specify whether the duckling belonged to the farmer or not (ibid.). That this choice is foreign to us shows that the way in which we conceive the scenario in language does not coincide with the way the Kwakiutl Indian conceives it.

Admittedly, the fact that few linguists are familiar with Kwakiutl does not simplify things for us, and we might feel obliged to agree with Sapir without having fully grasped the significance of his example. Let's take a simpler example from the Indo–European languages: Slavic languages demonstrate that they have no need of articles. In Czech, when one wants to stress that one has a single thing, one simply uses the word *one* (*jeden*, which, using the accusative form to imply possession), becomes *jednoho* in the following example, *I have a friend* (*Mám jednoho přítele*). Here we are insisting on the singularity of the friend. But most of the time, the concept of singularity is irrelevant because it is self-evident that we are concerned with one single noun. This reveals that the use of articles in English is largely conventional rather than intentional. This becomes obvious when we contrast the two following invitations: *Do you want a coffee? Do you want coffee?* In both questions the intention is clearly the same and it does not seem likely that the number of coffees enters into the mind of the speaker. At a subconscious level, however, Czech, in contrast to English, spares the speaker the choice of whether to use an article or not when it is semantically superfluous.

Languages handle concepts (even the simplest most concrete concepts such as coffee) using different grammatical constraints which condition the meaning of what we say. But a language is not simply the sum total of its concepts: language as a system is the interaction and the positioning of these individual concepts in relationship to one another. And it is because a language is a system within which we think that we are, to come back to Sapir's words in the above-mentioned quote, *at its mercy*: '. . . language, as a structure, is on its inner face the mold of thought' (Sapir 1949: 22). Thus, 'it is rather the tyranny of usage than the need of their concrete expression that sways us in the selection of this or that form' (1949: 98). For this reason, Sapir (in a rare use of personification) suggests that 'Language is in many respects . . . unreasonable and stubborn . . . Any concept that asks for expression must submit to the classificatory rules of the game . . .' (1949: 99).

One essential point should be made here, however: if language is *tyrannical* it is not the abstract system which is so, it is the weight of tradition which bears down upon the individual when he opens his mouth. Men have spoken before, and man copies the way they spoke, slipping into the 'formal grooves' they have traced, as cross-country skiers slip into the well-traced tracks left by those who have gone before them. The *tyranny in language* is then a human tyranny and not that of an impersonal structure. And it is for this very reason that the tyranny of usage can be resisted. In his consideration of 'the parts of speech', Sapir concludes that they reflect 'not so much our intuitive analysis of reality as our ability to compose that reality into a variety of formal patters' (1949: 118). Tyranny, paradoxically, does not seem to preclude freedom or variation in Sapir's conception of language. Perhaps this is best explained by the fact that Sapir never loses sight of the fact that language is a human product. If men had always been slaves to language, how could they have created it in the first place?

Wilhelm von Humboldt is famous for having rejected the idea of language as a *product*, claiming that it was an activity, a *producing*. In his distinction, he resituated the speaking man at the heart of language. Man conditions language, and language conditions man in an ongoing interactivity. Despite Sapir's use of the term *product*, of the trinity Boas-Sapir-Whorf, it is he who comes closest to this Humboldtian conception of the relationship between man and language. And it was the fact that he was highly attuned to language as an individual and deeply personal activity that allowed him to coin one of the best formulations in English of the relationship between thought and language: 'The instrument makes possible the product, the product refines the instrument' (Sapir, quoted by Lucy 1996: 20).

This formulation has the advantage of disrupting those misleadingly simplistic representations of language as either the subject or object in a causal relationship. Incessantly, linguists have sought to establish whether language conditions thought or vice versa, conceiving one of the terms as an active subject acting upon a passive object. Humboldt resists the reductive dehumanisation of *speaking* and *thinking* which is implicit in considering them in rigid nominal abstract terms as *speech* and *thought*. While speech and thought can easily be conceived of as objects in abstraction, speaking and thinking are ongoing activities which necessarily imply real individual speakers and thinkers. In the neat inversion above (the product that refines the instrument), Sapir takes a step in the direction of Humboldt's reanimated conception of language. Neither thought nor language is characterised in Sapir's work as a static object, a consequence of the other's intention.

If the relationship between thought and language is a mutually-influencing interactive one, it may seem vain to seek which comes first: just as the chicken implies the egg and vice versa, language and thought, in Sapir's model, seem to defy any attempt to find an origin. But this is somewhat misleading since Sapir clearly posits that language precedes thought and that thought can be considered an extension of language in the sense that it constitutes an interpretation of the classifications inherent and manifest in language:

From the point of view of language, thought may be defined as the highest latent or potential content of speech, the content that is obtained by interpreting each of the elements in the flow of language as possessed of its very fullest conceptual value.

[...] It is, indeed, in the highest degree likely that language is an instrument originally put to uses lower than the conceptual plane and that thought arises as a refined interpretation of its content. (Sapir, in Lucy 1996: 19–20)

This will no doubt appear confusing: How could thought be supposed to follow on from speech? Would that mean that we speak without thinking and that we learned to speak before thought became possible? Certainly, we all know people who tend to speak without seeming to think, but we generally find their behaviour annoying and aberrant because it makes communication extremely difficult. Is Sapir speculating about speech prior to the communication of ideas? This seems unlikely: in the above quote he is speaking about that reflective kind of thinking which includes reasoning and analysis, and which might be conceived as speech looking over its shoulder at itself. While there would seem to be no place outside language from which to analyse it in this model, we can, within the framework of a language system, stand back from aspects of our speech in order to analyse the way they function. In contrast, all speech implies thought, though most speech is spontaneous and intuitive rather than reflective. This posits two forms of thought: one, largely subconscious, a form of thought which the individual would find it difficult to separate from what he expresses in speech, the other, a conscious, reflexive, self-examining form of thought. And it is surely this second reflective, self-analysing thought which Sapir has in mind when he speaks of the *highest latent or potential content of speech*. Whether it takes place in the dialogues and conversations we have with others, or whether it takes place in the dialogues we have with ourselves in our minds, this refined form of reflection is of a paradoxical nature, because though it can be clearly distinguished from the act of speaking, it can only come into existence or be maintained by means of language.

Throughout his extensive analysis of various cases of conceptualisation, Sapir appears to be leading us to two conclusions according to Lucy:

> [. . .] we anticipate (or read) experience in terms of language categories which, by virtue of their abstraction and elaboration in the linguistic process, no longer correspond to experience in a direct way.
> It only remained to add to this the argument that these categories are only loosely equivalent to derive the conclusion that particular languages channel thought (i.e., conceptual interpretations of reality) in diverse ways. (Lucy 1996: 20)

This indeed seems to be Sapir's conclusion. Some degree of knowledge of the incommensurable analyses of experience to be found in different languages would bring home to us:

> . . . a kind of relativity that is generally hidden from us by our naïve acceptance of fixed habits of speech as guides to an objective understanding of the nature of experience. This is the relativity of concepts or, as it might be called, the relativity of the form of thought. (Sapir, quoted by Lucy 1996: 20–1)

Interestingly, however, Sapir rejected on empirical grounds the idea that culture and language were 'in any true sense causally related. Culture [he claimed] may be defined as *what* a society does and thinks. Language is a particular *how* of thought' (quoted by Lucy 1996: 22). Was Sapir trying to escape the tyranny of causal subject–object propositions which seek to derive culture from language or vice versa? Was he refusing to demote man, that creative, thinking, reflective animal, to the status of a pawn within a game governed by the will of one abstract force, depersonalised language? The answer to this remains unclear, but Sapir, for some reason, leads us towards the conclusion that language, as the product of human usage, governs thought, but then rejects the seemingly implicit consequence that thought will condition the culture we create. Doesn't the way we think (the *how*) bear upon *what* we think and do? Sapir's failure to provide a clear response is perplexing.

CHAPTER 6

Whorf

Accounts in English of the relationship between language and worldview and theories of linguistic relativity have tended to concentrate on Whorf's position, and consequently the influence of his work has been acknowledged more fully by scholars and studied in greater detail than either Boas' or Sapir's work. Perspicacious and stimulating accounts can be found in Malotki (1983), Lee (1996) and Lucy (1996), but if we are to understand the way thought concerning the relationship between language and worldview has tended to be limited to Whorf's ideas in debates in English-speaking circles, it will be necessary to give a brief outline of this linguist's ideas in the pages that follow.

Whorf's work is one of great scope and rigour. He takes us beyond the isolated concepts in language that Boas focused upon, he assimilates Sapir's idea of language as a system in which concepts and categories might be described as interwoven or might be said to position themselves in relation to one another. As early as the 1920s, Sapir had begun developing his concept of *patternment*: and this was to be of crucial importance for the development of Whorf's linguistic thought (Lee 1996: 34–53). Contrary to the inevitably atomistic bent of modern linguistics with its stress upon the specialised analysis of linguistic particulars in isolation from the act of speaking, Sapir (and later Whorf) underlined the importance of considering the meaning of each element of language within the context of the pattern as a whole. The individual word and the individual phoneme (*speech sound*, in Sapir's vocabulary, Lee 1996: 44) only took on meaning within context in its interaction with other words and sounds. For Sapir, each point was a point in a pattern. Sapir used a dance metaphor to explain this when he claimed that just as a movement of the foot only becomes *a step* once it is integrated into a dance, so a 'sound that is not unconsciously felt as "placed" with reference to other sounds is no more a true element of speech . . .' (Sapir in Lee 1996: 44).

From points in a pattern, Sapir went on to develop his concept of *clusters*. For Sapir, meaning formed into 'particular points or clusters of points of localization in the several tracts that refer to any element of language' (ibid.). These clusters were connected to the brain by association and they formed, in Sapir's opinion, '*a vast network of associated localization*' (ibid.). This was the idea that Whorf took up when he posited language as an interactive model of confronting planes of meaning. Whorf speaks frequently of *levels* and *planes* when he explains his conception of patternment, but, as one of the most enlightened Whorf scholars, Penny Lee, explains:

[. . .] it is clear that Whorf did not envisage these as separate in the sense that each one can be peeled off leaving an intact underlying layer exposed to view. Rather, they were conceptualized as interpenetrative, yet existing at the same time as fully self-contained systems. (1996: 39)

This demonstrates, Lee contends, 'Whorf's capacity to hold complex patterns of interconnections in mind at once and demonstrates his predilection to thinking in terms of wholes rather than parts' (ibid.).

Not only did Whorf take on board and develop Sapir's concept of patternment, though: in his plans at least, Whorf went much further. In his short article 'Language Plan and Conception of Arrangement', published in 1938 (Whorf [1956] 1984, edited by Carroll: 125–33), he proposed a meticulously clear project which would take in all aspects of language from the phoneme and the accent to rhetoric and conversation style. The plan was incredibly ambitious for any single linguist, and Whorf himself can hardly be blamed for not bringing the project to fruition in his own research. He did, however, always strive to make headway according to the plan and its clarity should remain an inspiration to others. In this sense, Whorf indicates the path to follow in conceiving the multiple aspects of language as the inseparable parts of one great whole.

Whorf himself concentrated primarily on what might be considered as deeper aspects of categorisation and conceptualisation than those treated by Sapir, and he was particularly interested in the ways space, time and matter are conceived in language. Though he is famous for his work on Hopi, a North American language, he also studied Hebrew, Aztec and Maya. The choice of the languages he studied was intentionally exotic. He argued:

> . . . the best approach is through an exotic language, for in its study we are at long last pushed willy-nilly out of our ruts. Then we will find that the exotic language is a mirror held up to our own. (Whorf, *The Relation of Habitual Thought and Behaviour to Language*, 1984: 138)

In trying to understand the organisation of the exotic language, Whorf reasoned, we will be forced to reappraise the conceptual categories of our own language. Reflection on the exotic will lead us to reflect upon the familiar with greater lucidity. In this sense, language study can be seen as a form of escape from the confines of our concepts. It is not by chance that where Boas speaks of *channels* and Sapir speaks of *grooves*, Whorf sees *ruts*. The mechanics of our own language are characterised by Whorf in terms of limits to be transcended. The spirit of Whorf's work was one of an adventurous exploration, and it was to this spirit that the cognitive linguist, George Lakoff, was responding when he described Whorf (in very American terms) as a *pioneer* (Lakoff 1987: 330).

Whorf's aim was to penetrate what he called the *thought world* of the exotic language. But what exactly did he mean by this term? In fact, this seems to be a synonym for various terms used by Whorf: *world-view*, *Weltanschauung* and *habitual thought*. He gave it the following definition:

> By 'habitual thought' and 'thought world' I mean more than simply language, i.e. than the linguistic patterns themselves. I include all the analogical and suggestive value of the patterns

(e.g., our 'imaginary space' and its distant implications), and all the give-and-take between language and the culture as a whole, wherein is a vast amount that is not linguistic but yet shows the shaping influence of language. In brief, this 'thought world' is the microcosm that each man carries about within himself, by which he measures and understands what he can of the macrocosm. (Whorf, *Habitual Thought . . .*, 1984: 147)

By contrasting Hopi and Indo-European languages (which he termed *Standard Average European* (*SAE*) Whorf 1984: 138), Whorf concluded that, 'The three-tense system of SAE verbs colors all our thinking about time' (143). The SAE system of verb forms was understood by Whorf as part of a larger scheme in which subjective experience was systematically objectified. This process of objectification tends to make us conceive of events and actions in terms of things happening in a sequence in space. 'This objectification [Whorf claimed] enables us in imagination to "stand time units in a row"' (ibid.).

Whorf's experience of Hopi as an exotic language had forced him out of this *rut*, and made him receptive to another conception of time. Indeed, he suggested that a binary conception of time which divided actions and events into earlier and later would 'correspond better to the feeling of duration as it is experienced' (ibid.). Whorf justified this claim in the following way:

For if we inspect consciousness we find no past, present, future, but a unity embracing complexity. EVERYTHING is in consciousness, and everything in consciousness is, and is together. There is in it a sensuous and a nonsensuous. We may call the sensuous – what we are seeing, hearing, touching – the 'present' while in the nonsensuous the vast image-world of memory is being labelled 'the past' and another realm of belief, intuition, and uncertainty 'the future'; yet sensation, memory, foresight, all are in consciousness together – one is not 'yet to be' nor another 'once but no more'. (1984: 143–4)

Back at the beginning of the fifth century, in Book 12 of his *Confessions*, Saint Augustine was preoccupied with this very question, when he confessed to God that time remained for him a great mystery. 'I know that I confess it, Lord, and that it is in time that I say these things [. . .] Alas, I do not know what I do not know' (1964b: chapter XXV, 274, mT). Augustine found himself caught in a paradox:

I measure time, I know. But I do not measure the future which is not yet come, I do not measure the present, for it has no length, do not measure the past, because it is no longer here. What do I measure, then? Is it time as it passes and not the time once past as I have already said? (1964b: chapter XXVI, 275–6, mT)

That time remained a mystery for Augustine would have come as little surprise to Whorf, because he contended that the specialised systems of science and philosophy tended to be constructed out of the same system as everyday concepts. As such, they could be considered as sophisticated elaborations of habitual thought patterns. Was Augustine simply clawing at the confines of his *thought world*? If he had read Augustine, how would Whorf have understood his dilemma? Would he have congratulated himself, on his return from the Hopi *thought world*, that this exotic language had enabled him to transcend the conception that confined the philosopher? Certainly, for Augustine, since God exists outside time, having brought it into existence himself at the same time as He made creation, escaping time would have to be considered a divine act. Nor would Augustine (who for many years worked as a teacher of rhetoric) have seen any contradiction between the intellectual analysis of reality on the one hand, and time and language and spirituality on the other, since in his Christian conception of man, the intellectual soul was the god-like gift God endows man with to help him come to a closer knowledge of the divine.

Whorf's work is of a very different nature, however: it was forged from the materialist mechanics and dynamics of cause and effect common to most nineteenth- and twentieth-century positivist thought. But in trying to escape our language and move beyond (or rise above) the confines of our thought world, Whorf was yearning towards spiritual questions (as can be seen from his attraction for yoga and Indian culture). And one noteworthy consequence of this duality is that it allows us to reinvest the spirit with the intellectual and analytical capacity which Christian thinkers of the Classical and Medieval periods such as both Augustine and Aquinas attributed to the spirit, though the relationship between analysis and spirituality has been obscured to a great degree since the Enlightenment and the Church went their separate ways.

In Whorf's concept of the thought world, language and metaphysics were inextricably bound up together. The *Hopi thought world*, in contrast to our tripartite time-scape was based upon two principles: 'two grand cosmic forms, which as a first approximation in terminology we may call MANIFESTED and MANIFESTING (or UNMANIFEST)' (Whorf, *An American Indian Model of the Universe*, 1984: 59).

In his use of parts of speech to describe language, Whorf (like Humboldt) strove to avoid nouns. This is an active resistance to the routine representation of activities (verbs) as things. In English, actions taken out of the context of occurring tend to be conceived as separate entities. In opposition to this, Whorf chose to describe things that happen in Hopi not as *events* but as *eventing*. Of course, few people would accept that *eventing* is an English word. But this was precisely Whorf's intention: to allow the thought world of Hopi to expand the horizons of the habitual thought patterns of English. *Eventing* implied a conception of the transformation and metamorphosis of things, not so much in terms of objects and outside forces which act upon them, as developing processes which were the consequence of some internal, organic growing. The following passage explains this in terms of a *preparedness* which appertains to each action or changing thing:

> [. . .] both the physical and nonphysical events are considered the expression of invisible intensity factors, on which depend their stability and persistence, or their fugitiveness and proclivities. It implies that existents do not 'become later and later' all in the same way; but some do so by growing like plants, some by diffusing and vanishing, some by a procession of metamorphoses, some by enduring in one shape till affected by violent forces. In the nature of each existent able to manifest as a definite whole is the power of its own mode of

duration: its growth, decline, stability, cyclicity, or creativeness. Everything is thus already 'prepared' for the way it now manifests by earlier phases, and what it will be later, partly has been, and partly is in the act of being so 'prepared'. An emphasis and importance rests on this preparing or being prepared aspect of the world that may to the Hopi correspond to that 'quality of reality' that 'matter' or 'stuff' has for us. (*Habitual Thought*, 1984: 147–8)

Curiously, despite the fact that Whorf tends to consider philosophy as no more than an extension of language-bound conceptual thought, the idea that metamorphosis can be conceived in terms of the inherent, intrinsic and ever-present property of things corresponds closely to ideas expressed by Aristotle in his definition of form (*The Physics*, Book IV). While modern materialism tends to concentrate our attention upon the physical make-up of things (what Aristotle defined as *matter*, or rather the *material cause* in his distinction of form and matter), each thing is subject to what Aristotle called the *fourth cause*, the teleological destiny which things carry within themselves; their end or *raison d'être*. To quote one example, the acorn carries within itself the need to realise itself by becoming an oak. Whether it achieves this goal or not does not change the fact that its need to become something which transcends its present form is inscribed within it, and animates it.

While Boas moved from the cultural to the linguistic, Whorf's preoccupation with the fundamental grammar of languages led him into metaphysical speculation. Grammar is essential to the meaning we give to things and to experience. This is one essential point that must be made in the light of the importance that grammar has been accorded by generative linguists following Noam Chomsky from the 1960s onwards. While generative linguistics tends to formalise language and bracket the question of meaning, for Whorf:

The very essence of linguistics is the quest for meaning, and, as the science refines its procedure, it inevitably becomes, as a matter of this quest, more psychological and cultural, while retaining that almost mathematical precision of statement which it gets from the highly systematic nature of the linguistic realm of fact. (Whorf, *A Linguistic Consideration of the Thinking in Primitive Communities*, 1984: 79)

What interests Whorf is how linguistic communities make sense of the world. The meaning the world has for people, and the way they speak about it and work within it, are all bound up together for Whorf. And at times, Whorf goes as far as to suggest that thought, language and behaviour coincide. We can see this if we return to our example of time and *eventing*.

Our behaviour, and that of Hopi, can be seen to be coordinated in many ways to the linguistically conditioned microcosm [. . .] A characteristic of Hopi behaviour is the emphasis on preparation. This includes announcing and getting ready for events well beforehand, elaborate precautions to insure persistence of desired conditions, and stress on good will as the preparer of right results [. . .] This is the way the Hopi deal with the future – by working within a present situation which is expected to carry impresses, both obvious and occult, forward into the future event of interest. (Whorf, *Habitual Thought*, 1984: 148)

Those of us who have no knowledge of the Amerindian language, Hopi, must guard against judging the specific nature of preparations for the future in this culture, but as far as Whorf's argument goes that the exotic language will plunge us into a thought world of an entirely different order, the above example seems rather weak evidence. Are there any European cultures in which elaborate preparations for great occasions are not to be found? In Europe and North America, it will often take one year to arrange a wedding and invite all of the members of the family to express their good will and best wishes: is this to be understood as something essentially Hopi in our cultures?

If the evidence Whorf provides for the link between thought and behaviour is weak, what can be said about the relationship between language and culture? On this point there seems to be some confusion: though both are considered to form part of the thought world, Whorf did in fact claim that he would be the last person 'to pretend there is anything so definite as "a correlation" between culture and language' (Whorf 1984: 139). So, in terms of the three primary questions concerning the influence of language on behaviour, culture and perception, Whorf provides little argument and evidence to support a deterministic role for language, at least for the first two questions, behaviour and culture. What does he have to say about the third, perception?

Lucy claims that 'the evidence that he [Whorf] believed that language directly influences perception is slender and inconsistent' (Lucy 1996: 42). Lucy explains that Whorf considered the external world to be essentially unstructured from the point of view of the speaker, and quotes his use of terms such as, '"stream of sensory experience," "raw experience," "kaleidoscopic flux of impressions," "flux of experience," "mass of presentation," "flowing face of nature," and "continuous spread and flow of existence"' (ibid.). Some of these expressions give a very vivid picture (or scenario) of the nature of experience that Whorf was trying to evoke. Others, such as 'the flowing face of nature' have the clumsy feel of mixed metaphors. Perhaps 'continuous spread and flow of existence' catches best of all the ongoing activity of the world around us. It is reminiscent of the view of one pre-Socratic Greek philosopher, Heraclitus (540–480 BC). The view of Heraclitus, according to which all reality was subject to a constant state of flux, was largely interred when Plato (429–347 BC) sided with Parmenides (540–450 BC) in privileging the eternal unchanging aspect of nature over the transitory and the changing. Western metaphysics and science has, at any rate, tended to follow Plato in searching for and attempting to uncover unchanging truths of the world.

Whorf's perspective was helping him to focus on things differently. He was taking a great step when he chose to refocus the language debate on verbs rather than nouns. Philosophers had long since established that words were not things but concepts. John Locke in *An Essay Concerning Human Understanding* (first published in 1689), made this distinction clear: 'Words, in their primary or immediate signification, stand for nothing but *the ideas in the mind of him that uses them*' (Locke 1964: 259, original italics). They are, Locke claimed, necessary for communication in which they will be used to designate actual things, but they do not bear any fixed relation to any actual physical thing in the world around us. Things are, of course, in any case, too numerous to be named. And even if we could name them all, what would be the use of categories which included a single member?

Still, despite his sensitivity to the mental construction of lexical categories, most of Locke's discussion of language was restricted to the consideration of nouns (concrete and abstract) and the English philosophical tradition has tended to approach the question of the relationship between words and things by talking about the names of things, i.e. nouns. Relational words such as prepositions and activities (verbs) have received much less treatment by philosophers, if any. This has resulted in a distorted picture of what language is and of how we use it to talk of our experience in the world around us.

Philosophy's reductive fixation on nouns would tend to confirm Whorf's intuition that philosophy is derived from an extension of the conceptual patterns found in our language since our European languages (and especially French) have tended to accord the noun a central position in language. This question would require far greater investigation than is possible here, however. We should restrict ourselves, therefore, to pointing out that Whorf is not altogether unfair when he expresses frustration with logicians who limit their investigation of the relationship between words and reality to discussions of tables and chairs, isolated, man-made artefacts. Things like tables and chairs do exist to a large degree in isolation and it would be reasonable to expect language to treat them in this way. But most language, Whorf stressed, was not like this. Neither, for that matter, was our perception and experience of reality limited to things. For this reason Whorf asserted:

> The real question is: What do different languages do, not with these artificially isolated objects but with the flowing face of nature in its motion, color, and changing form. . .? (Whorf, in Lucy 1996: 42)

Was Whorf defending the idea that languages condition perception? To some degree it would seem that his research on temporality led him to believe that we conceive things in language. But he seems to have felt that experience of reality was largely universal: at least his comments on whether Hopi corresponds better to our perception of time would lead us to presume that both English-speakers and Hopi Indians experience the same kaleidoscopic flux of experience.

His arguments do not appear to defend a relativistic idea that the way we perceive the world depends upon the language we speak. The world, presumably, remains the world for both English-speakers and Hopi Indians. What is Whorf defending, then? If Whorf is defending something, then it is more the idea that the Hopi language and thought world correspond more closely to our shared world. At times, Whorf adopts the worldly open-mindedness of Boas' relativism, when he talks about the equal efficiency with which languages handle experience. This can be seen, for example, when he claims that 'the Hopi language gets along perfectly without tenses for its verbs' (Whorf 1984: 64).

At other times, it is clear that Whorf is claiming that Hopi allows us a privileged insight into the true nature of reality. This is evidenced by the following statement: 'Hopi can have verbs without subjects, and this gives to that language power as a logical system for understanding certain aspects of the cosmos' (1984: 263). Indo-European languages have caused us to fall under the illusion of taking our words for things. And this reification can be seen to reach back into the way we experience the world by seeking to formulate that experience in terms of nouns, seeking out actions where in fact what we experience might better described in terms of a state (ibid.). Whorf logically concludes: 'the road out of illusion for the West lies through a wider understanding of language than western Indo-European alone can give' (ibid.).

Whorf's relativism, it would appear, is often far from relativistic. Statements like the one above bring him closer to the evolutionist view of languages found in Schleicher and Hovelacque with their hierarchies of superior and inferior languages than to Sapir and Boas. Indeed, Whorf himself might be said to be as fluid as the verb forms he analyses: he moves between a relativist position and a staunch stance in defence of the objective superiority of Hopi. How are we to understand the following statement if not as a rejection of relativism?

Does the Hopi language show here a higher plane of thinking, a more rational analysis of situations, than our vaunted
English? Of course it does. In this field [sensation] and in
various others, English, compared to Hopi is like a bludgeon
compared to a rapier. (Whorf, *A Linguistic Consideration of
Thinking in Primitive Communities*, 1984: 85)

This is not the tone of Boas' and Sapir's tentative hypotheses. As
Jewish Germans, their travel between languages and worldviews
formed part of their everyday linguistic, mental and emotional lives:
Whorf adopts the tone of a convert in this quote. While Boas and
Sapir both counter the prevailing linguistic racism of their time,
Whorf slips ungracefully into inverting it and championing the
underdog, claiming that its subtlety far outreaches that of the dominant language, English. Those of us who do not speak Hopi should
refrain from discounting the advantages of the Hopi worldview since
we simply do not have access to the knowledge necessary to form
an opinion. We might, however, be justified in viewing the above
statement with the same scepticism that we view those attempts to
rehabilitate the Indian in films of recent decades in which the *savage*
is transformed into a Hollywood version of Rousseau's *noble savage*.

It is not only Whorf's conclusions which prove questionable.
A contemporary commentator on linguistic relativism Zdenek
Salzmann queries the reliability of Whorf's illustrations (Salzmann
1999: 64), because Whorf relied for his examples on a bilingual
informant who lived in New York. Did Whorf's knowledge of
Hopi really suffice to allow him entry into the thought world of that
language? And for all the rigour of his research and the ardour with
which Whorf yearned to penetrate a different worldview, is there
not some degree of naivety in his quest to find some kind of solution
to Western metaphysics in the thought world of Hopi? If so, then
Whorf falls into the same wishful thinking as the French writer,
Anne Stamm, who in her research sought an African spirituality,
presumably as solace for those who believe themselves to be living
in what many European intellectuals consider to be the spiritually
bankrupt West.

The reception Stamm and Whorf received is in no way comparable, however. While Stamm, writing at the turn of the twenty-first

century in France, will find many sympathisers, the reception of Whorf has been considerably more problematic: Whorf was both celebrated and censured in his own country. The most radical of his affirmations have invariably been selected by both supporters and critics, and he has tended to be reduced to these positions. There is a perverse justice in this, since linguists are only doing to Whorf what he himself did to Sapir in selecting for quotation the most deterministic of Sapir's phrases notably that we 'are at the mercy of the language' we speak (Sapir quoted by Whorf 1984: 134).

The upshot of this selective and reductive quotation has been that the strong form of the Sapir-Whorf hypothesis (which practically eclipses Sapir) has tended to persist and Whorf himself has all too often been characterised as a dogmatic thinker who believed that languages were like prisons from which we cannot escape. This is a grotesque misrepresentation of Whorf's view of language, a view which he resumed in the following passage:

> [. . .] thinking is most mysterious, and by far the greatest light upon it that we have is thrown by the study of language. The study shows that the forms of a person's thoughts are controlled by inexorable laws of pattern of which he is unconscious. These patterns are the unperceived intricate systematizations of his own language – shown readily enough by a candid comparison and contrast with other languages especially those of a different linguistic family. His thinking itself is in a language – in English, in Sanskrit, in Chinese. And every language is a vast pattern-system, different from others, in which are culturally ordained the forms and categories by which the personality not only communicates, but also analyzes nature, notices or neglects types of relationship and phenomena, channels his reasoning, and builds the house of his consciousness. (*Language Thought and Reality*, 1984: 252)

Houses of consciousness are not prisons. Nevertheless, it is the parody of Whorf that has tended to be held up – and then knocked down. Though European scholars are often inclined to invoke the *Sapir-Whorf hypothesis*, Whorf has become a straw man for contemporary

Anglo-American linguistics. As the contemporary specialist of metaphor, the Berkeley linguist, George Lakoff suggests:

> For the past few decades, most 'respectable' scholars have steered clear of relativism. It has become a bête noire, identified with scholarly irresponsibility, fuzzy thinking, lack of rigor, and even immorality. Disavowals and disproofs are de rigueur [. . .] In many circles even the smell of relativism is tainted. (1987: 304)

For the French readers of Stamm, such a statement will be all but incomprehensible. Moral correctness in France reposes (in theory at least, and in intellectual circles) on the principles of openness and relativism. And any antipathy to moral relativism tends to be classified by most French intellectuals as American Puritanism, a view which Americans will probably find just as absurd as Stamm's readers will find the antipathy to alternative world-views absurd. Lakoff does stress that there are those who have championed relativism in North America, but his own defence of relativism, 'Alternative conceptual systems exist, whether one likes it or not' (1987: 336), implies that most Americans do not share his enthusiasm.

Curiously, the majority of books being produced on the question of worldviews in the English-speaking world are defences of the Christian faith, and ultimately defences of one worldview over others (the *true Christian worldview* as opposed to false worldviews). This has not prevented contemporary American Christian thinkers such as James W. Sire and especially David K. Naugle from making contributions to research concerning the philological and philosophical origins of the term *worldview*. Nevertheless, faith can hardly spur on the quest into alternative linguistic systems of consciousness, and Christian dogma does seem fundamentally irreconcilable with Whorf's idea that philosophy can never go beyond a more complex manipulation of the fundamental patterns of thought available to the speakers of any language. Faith in the Gospel, for the Christian, transcends language. Consequently, Christian antipathy towards linguistic relativism may well have contributed to the fact that a caricature of Whorf's work has been allowed to mask the true subtlety and erudition of his work down to the present day.

Moreover, it would be absurd to seek a simple explanation for why Whorf's thought has been marginalised and misrepresented. And if he does seem to have been swept aside, a conspiracy theory would hardly explain why this has happened. Indeed, several elements seem to have converged to exclude Whorf. The political and intellectual climate in which Whorf's ideas were being aired must be remembered.

The Cold War was a period in which American linguistics pursued form over meaning. As we have seen, this goes against the very definition of linguistics Whorf gave, and such an intellectual climate can hardly have been conducive to the contemplation of his ideas. Increasingly during the Cold War, *the American way of life* was contrasted with the sad existence of oppressed Communists. On the Western side (we liked to believe) was freedom of thought: on the other was propaganda and the manipulation of the individual. A period in which the collective unconscious was shaped by films such as the *Invasion of the Body Snatchers* (a film which portrayed free-spirited Americans having their minds taken over by alien powers) can hardly have been the ideal setting in which to promote a linguistics open to alternative worldviews. Freedom of thought for the individual, in the Cold War politicized use of the concept, was so highly prized at the time of McCarthy's purge, that the idea that we are somehow controlled or limited by language can hardly have seemed palatable. Tastes are fickle and impressions are vague, but both the tastes and impressions of the Cold War may go some way towards explaining why Whorf's ideas were passed over, simply went out of fashion, were resented or actively marginalised. Certainly Penny Lee in the 1990s is justified in arguing that the contribution that Whorf made to linguistic thinking, a contribution which grew out of the fertile soil of the Prague Linguistics Circle and American university debates in the first half of the century, contrasts sharply with the way linguistic thinking was ignored in the second half of the century (Lee 1996: 35).

The concept of worldview was born into a very different intellectual and cultural climate. The thought of eighteenth-century Germany which contributed to the cultivation of Humboldt's mind (and indirectly influenced the thought of his two country-men, Boas and Sapir) was animated by a dual concern for the individual and the nation. In the thought of Jean Gottlieb Herder (1744–1803), thought which influenced the great writers of his time and of subsequent generations (Goethe and Hegel among others), the striving of the individual to create himself within language was held to be a part of the thrust of the nation towards a higher level of culture. The Cold War, in contrast, was perhaps the most extreme example of the separation of the individual and society. While Communist countries represented culture and history as the movement of societies in which individuals should recognise their historical role and serve it, capitalist countries tended to see culture as the affair of individuals who should be wary of interfer-ence from wider social groups or from the state. The individual who sets himself against (corrupt) society (the fantasy upon which so many of Hollywood's scenarios were based) was considered by many people in Communist countries as a form of perverted decadent individualism.

In championing the independent, free-thinking, unfettered indi-vidual, post-war America can hardly have been the ideal soil in which Whorf's idea of the collective thought world could take root. In such a period, any idea that seemed to imply that thought is con-ditioned by language must have appeared as a variation on George Orwell's Newspeak (the state's attempt to limit the individual's thought to the party line of the totalitarian regime).

Whorf tended to stress the influence of language on the indi-vidual's conception of the world, but offered little comment on the fact that language is the work of man (or rather men and women interacting in ongoing relationships in space and time). The model of language which Herder and Humboldt were working with was one of an evolving language with man evolving within it: it was a dynamic model. But in twentieth-century North America, this model was eclipsed by the reduction of Boas' and Sapir's positions to Whorf's own stance and to a simplification of the latter's thought. The result is ironic: Whorf, the champion of fluid experience, has been transformed into the major if not the sole representative of a static model of language which conditions and constricts the move-ment of man's thought.

As we shall see in the following chapters, this is a very different conception of worldview from the one elaborated by the linguist held to have introduced the term, Humboldt. Clearly, if the concept of worldview is to be of any use in understanding the relationship between language and thought, we must retrace it to its origins in his work. Though it would be interesting to examine in greater detail the work of both Sapir and Whorf, and though this would indeed help us to escape the limitations of the representation of worldview as it has come to be used by both opponents and defenders of the Sapir-Whorf hypothesis, going further into their work would not help us to grasp the original impetus which gave penetrating force and poignancy to this term, because often both Sapir and Whorf seem to be struggling to express ideas which had already been formulated by Humboldt over a hundred years before. Though Sapir may have been familiar with some of Humboldt's work, it does not play any great role in organising his thought. Whorf scholars have yet to make any convincing case for a link between him and Humboldt. On the whole, it seems likely that if there is any continuity between the ideas to be found in the works of Humboldt, Sapir and Whorf, then it can be explained by the fact that all three had their roots in the eighteenth-century German tradition which affirmed that language was the organ of thought. Humboldt was brought up in that tradition. Boas and Sapir introduced it into the American tradition, and Whorf adopted it (almost as dogma). It seems unlikely, however, that Sapir or Whorf borrowed it directly from Humboldt.

Part II: Humboldt, Man and Language

CHAPTER 7

Worldview (*Weltanschauung* or *Weltansicht*)

W ho was Wilhelm von Humboldt, this thinker who contemplated languages and tried to draw some bold conclusions about their nature and the nature of speech itself? He was born Baron Karl Wilhelm von Humboldt in 1767 in Potsdam, Prussia. Jürgen Trabant, a present-day German Humboldt specialist, begins his *Humboldt ou le sens de langage* (*Humboldt or the Sense of Language*, published in 1992) by quoting the impression Humboldt made upon the French romantic poet, Chateaubriand. For the poet, Humboldt was a quiet man who would withdraw from society 'to kill time by learning all the languages of the world and even their patois' (Trabant 1992: 14, mT). For poets enamoured of the Byronic ideal, Humboldt did not seem to cut a very dashing figure. True, he was in Paris only ten years after the French revolution, a time of great social and philosophical turmoil; true he was the friend of two of the greatest German poets of the time, Schiller and Goethe. His career was hardly that of a failure: though Prussia was suffering from defeats in the Napoleonic wars, Humboldt himself played an important political role during the period as a Director for the Ministry of Culture (1809–1810) and as Ambassador (1810–1819), first in Vienna, then London, before returning to the same post in Vienna.

Still, that would hardly suffice to make him the pillar of philology that certain thinkers have considered him to be (Heidegger, Chomsky, Meschonnic, Trabant, Langham Brown, Hansen-Løve et al.). And if his political actions were his main contribution to history, and if, as Chateaubriand seems to suggest, his work with language was merely a hobby, a pastime, he would perhaps deserve no more than the cursory treatment that David Crystal accords him in his encyclopaedia as the wordsmith who coined the term *worldview*. Yet even this claim to posterity is questionable. For what word did Crystal have in mind as the German term for *worldview*? Thinking within the conceptual framework of the Sapir-Whorf hypothesis, Crystal most probably had in mind *Weltanschauung*. As we have seen, Humboldt used this term at the beginning of the nineteenth century, as did Whorf himself a hundred years later. But Humboldt was not the first to do so. Indeed, Naugle, in *Worldview: The History of a Concept* (2002) quotes James Orr (a little-known Christian thinker of the late nineteenth century) who attributes the term to the great eighteenth-century philosopher Emmanuel Kant (1724–1804) who preceded Humboldt by almost two generations. For Kant, *Weltanschauung* is related to his idea of *world concept* (*Weltbegriff*). In Naugle's words, *Weltanschauung* 'functioned as an idea of pure reason to bring the totality of human experience into the unity of the world-whole, or *Weltganz*' (*sic*, Naugle 2002: 9; the correct term would appear to be *das Weltganze*). Naugle points out, however, that the term *Weltanschauung* is rarely used by Kant (or later romantic philosophers such as Fichte and Schelling). It did, though, because of the phenomenal influence of Kantian philosophy, become a central term for 'focusing on the human mind about which the world orbited' (ibid.). Hegel was one of the many thinkers to adopt it in the following decades when he used the term in his investigation of the way in which a man's *Weltanschauung* is linked to his religion or to philosophical knowledge.

By the last quarter of the nineteenth century, Orr observed that the concept of worldview had become common currency in books dealing with religion and philosophy. The Jewish German philologist, Victor Klemperer, records in his notes on the language of the Nazis (published as *LTI* in 1957) how he was amazed by the transformation of the term. *Weltanschauung* had taken wing from its nest in a restricted neo-Romantic intellectual discourse of the turn of the century, to become a by-word for every Nazi party member, every petty bourgeois, every shopkeeper (Klemperer 1975: 185). The Nazis, it would seem, were eager to defend the idea that they too had their vision of the world, a radiant vision, shared by each and every party member.

Naugle's book traces the trajectory of the term *Weltanschauung* as it is adapted in various discourses from Kant, through German philosophy and up to existentialist twentieth-century thought. Klemperer's study of the transformation of German political discourse and everyday conversation reveals the way language and ideology are bound up together. But in stressing the philosophical and ideological importance of worldview-as-*Weltanschauung* we are forgetting the other half of the worldview-concept, *Weltansicht*, the concept which forms the cornerstone of Humboldt's linguistic philosophy.

Let's return to the distinction that Trabant made between *Weltansicht* and *Weltanschauung* in disentangling the various attempts that had been made by linguists, philosophers and thinkers to understand Humboldt's work. Trabant asserted that worldviews (*Weltanschauungen*) were visions of the world in the sense of conceptions or ideologies. They were affirmations about the nature of the world and our place within it. In contrast to this, for Humboldt:

> languages are not assemblages of *affirmations* about the world which we hold to be true. Languages affirm nothing about the world; they give us the world in a certain way, thereby allowing assertive discourses (among others) upon the nature of the world. (Trabant 1992: 56, mT)

An example will help to clarify this point. A communist worldview might clash with, or exclude, a capitalist worldview. Both might be condemned as distorted or perverted perspectives by a Christian, just as a Catholic might condemn New Age Protestant cults and the worldviews they promote. And yet, all of these radically different visions of the world might take root and fight for territory within the same linguistic community. Furthermore, any one of the above belief-systems has grown and thrived in a multiplicity of languages of very different types, so even though they would appear to be conceptually constrictive, they are, unquestionably, linguistically flexible. *Weltansichten*, on the other hand, are language-bound. A *Weltansicht* constitutes the individual form or nature of the language (but also, in a deeper sense, its meaning too). A worldview-as-*Weltansicht* is the capacity which language bestows upon us to form the concepts with which we think and which we need in order to communicate.

Whorf may have used the term *Weltanschauung* when he evoked his concept of thought worlds, but what he had in mind was closer to *Weltansicht*. And so, by a strange quirk of logic, Crystal, in attributing the concept of worldview to Humboldt, was not mistaken: for it is in Humboldt's thought that this term is born and reaches fruition, as a fully developed concept. It was his concept (*Weltansicht*) that emerged in a stunted form in Whorf's thought. A direct link between Whorf and Humboldt seems untenable: Whorf's terminology and the concepts he uses seem to link him into a German post-Kantian tradition (especially his use of terms such as 'a noumenal world' (Lee 1996: 40). But his vision of language was that of a Kantian Visionary, someone who believed that language study would open up 'a world of hyper-space, of higher dimensions' which awaited the discovery by all the sciences. The tone of Humboldt's linguistic philosophy was entirely different. This is not so much a question of personality as one of epoch: Whorf is a twentieth-century thinker trying to reach across the barriers we have erected between disciplines. His holistic bent is both radical and unorthodox. Humboldt was writing in a century when the links between science, language, thought and philosophy were self-evident for his contemporaries. Whorf's fertile thought might have blossomed into something deeper, but with his untimely death and a context hostile to linguistic diversity, it went to seed. His promising concept of thought world was vulgarised into the Sapir-Whorf hypothesis, and it became only too easy to represent that hypothesis as radical, unfounded and absurd.

The story of *Weltansicht* as a concept (worldview as the configuration of concepts which allow conceptual thought) was a short-lived story in English-speaking countries. The protagonist had hardly entered on stage before he was pushed into the shadows, and finally dismissed. As the ideological and metaphysical concept of worldview (*Weltanschauung*) waxed strong in both Germany and in the US, *Weltansicht* waned within the linguistic project. Even the most erudite and reliable of Whorf scholars, such as Penny Lee, though they speak of *the Humboldt tradition*, do so without quoting Humboldt. The consequence of this *Humboldtless Humboldt tradition* is inevitable: the concept of worldview is invariably confused in English-speaking countries with the term *Weltanschauung* (Lee 1996: 84). In the US of Whorf's time and throughout the second half of the twentieth century, *Weltansicht* – language as the capacity to coin concepts – was scarcely a welcome extra in the scenario of linguistics. And linguists interested in Whorf's intuitions – weak echoes of Humboldt's voice – were forced to critically reappraise linguistic relativism in order to reinstate it as an academically respectable position (Lakoff 1987: 304).

CHAPTER 8

Sprache

Before examining more fully the concept of *Weltansicht* as it appears in Humboldt's work, we should first try to grasp the innovative conception of language that Humboldt worked with. Humboldt spoke of language (*Sprache*) in very vivid organic terms: and this was not simply a stylistic flourish. On the contrary, the organic imagery with which he thought of language and with which he sought to disentangle himself from other organic and inorganic metaphoric representations of language, were part of his conception of the faculty of speech as the *formative organ of thought*. The two main representations of language from which Humboldt was trying to liberate himself were those of the vehicle model and the mirror model of language. For most philosophers of the Enlightenment (and Humboldt remained in many respects a proponent of the Enlightenment project which sought to discover the nature of man), language was considered to be the creation of human Reason. It may be a necessary outward vehicle, philosophers supposed, for Reason's more complex operations, but it remained subordinate to Reason (Langham Brown 1967: 58). The German Enlightenment philosopher, Leibniz (1646–1716), a major influence on Humboldt, went so far as to suggest that words could 'help our own thoughts' (ibid.), but he conceived language basically as 'the mirror of the intellect' (57). Language reflects thought, it was argued. The anthropologist, Franz Boas, two hundred years later, was working with very much the same idea when he investigated the way the language of the Amerindians revealed their culture. And Sapir and Whorf never fully escaped this mode of representing language.

But already in the middle of the 1700s an alternative representation of the relationship between thought and language was emerging to challenge the enlightened view of language as a useful tool for expressing thought. Indeed the image itself of language as the *organ of thought* was not coined by Humboldt but inherited from Jean-Georges Hamann and Herder (Berlin, Langham Brown, Steiner, Trabant et al.). Hamann (1830–1888), Herder's contemporary, had already asserted that 'the entire capacity to think rests on language' (quoted by Langham Brown 1967: 61). For this reason Hamann felt sure that language must have come before thought. One belief that Humboldt shared with his precursor, Herder, and which was developed by Hamann was the idea that: 'the differences between languages parallel differences in ways of thought' (Hamann, quoted by Langham Brown 1967: 61). Hamann had already asserted: 'The lineaments [of a people's] language will also correspond to the direction of their sort of thinking' (ibid.). Herder's thought on language was moving in a similar direction and he seems to be expressing an idea similar to Whorf's thought world, when he contended that 'Human language carries its *thought forms* in itself; we think especially when we think abstractly, only in and with language' (Langham Brown 1967: 62).

So what did Humboldt bring to the concept of language? Humboldt radically developed the concept in two ways. The first way concerned the speaking man that perpetuates language. The second way was his adoption and adaptation of Kant's reappraisal of perception.

Humboldt conceptualised language not as a fixed, unchanging *thing* but as a living process. While language endures, it only endures because we live within it. Language is sustained in any semi-permanent form only by the transitory acts of speaking and writing carried out by people everyday (Humboldt 1999: 49). Even when we conceive of a language as something belonging to a community, Humboldt insisted, we should not forget that it remains personal and present. We have no contact with language that does not involve speaking men or words written by them.

This way of thinking about language encouraged Humboldt to make a crucial break with philosophies which conceived of languages as products of society and objects of study. Though a great deal of his philological work was textual, Humboldt stressed the importance of the spoken word: this, for Humboldt, was the locus for study and he saw written texts as an extension of man's presence in language. For this reason he asserted:

> Even its [language's] maintenance by writing is always just an incomplete, mummy-like preservation, only needed again in attempting thereby to picture the living utterance. In itself it [language] is no product (*Ergon*), but an activity (Energeia). (ibid.)

As we have already seen, Humboldt contended that language should be conceived of as a *producing* (*Erzeugung*), rather than as a *dead product* (*todtes Erzeugtes*) (2003: 314). Grammarians and lexicographers, while essential for the linguistic project, were relegated to a secondary role in Humboldt's project, for they could only browse the bones of language, or at best cut up its dead abstract corpse. For Humboldt, the real thrust of philology lay in penetrating the function of language as 'a designator of objects and instrument of understanding' (1999: 48). Language was closely entwined with 'inner mental activity' (as Heath translates *Geistesthätigkeit*). And this *Geistesthätigkeit* was conceived of as an energetic creative force which works upon language as men carve their ideas into expression but which simultaneously works upon the minds of men as they adopt and adapt the creative expression that is handed down to them in speech.

If Humboldt argued that the study of this inner mental activity required close attention to detail, it was because:

> Language presents us with an infinity of *details*, in words, rules, analogies and exceptions of every kind, and we are not a little perplexed at how to bring this mass, which, apart from the order already brought into it, still seems to us a bewildering chaos, into judicious comparison with the unity of the image of man's *mental power*. (ibid.)

It was the linguist's vocation to understand how man's mental power (*die menschliche Geisteskraft*, 2003: 314) managed to create meaning from these chaotic details. He should prise from this activity an idea of the nature of the process by which meaning was formed from individual parts. He could, Humboldt argued, 'thereby endeavour to catch the character' of different branches of languages (1999: 48). But however important this study of details was, a knowledge of lexical and grammatical elements in and for themselves did not aid much in this endeavour, Humboldt explained:

> Um daher verschiedne [*sic*] Sprachen in Bezug auf ihren charakteristischen Bau fruchtbar mit einander zu vergleichen, muss man der Form einer jeden derselben sorgfältig nachforschen und sich auf diese Weise vergewissern, auf welche Art jede die hauptsächlichen Fragen löst, welche aller Spracherzeugung als Aufgaben vorliegen. (2003: 314–15)

> So, in order to compare different languages fruitfully with one another, in regard to their characteristic structure, we must carefully investigate the form of each, and in this way ascertain how each resolves the main questions with which all language-creation is confronted. (1999: 48)

This passage has been quoted in German to highlight the use of the words *Bau* and *Form*, which Heath translates respectively as *structure* and *form*. It is important to avoid any confusion with later uses of the term *structure* by Structuralists in France and English-speaking countries. *Bau*, for Humboldt, implies construction and construction implies, in turn, a constructor or constructors. Whether the speaking individual is expressing himself in a new and original manner, or whether he is relying on the paths opened up to him by established speech, Humboldt's model of language never eclipses the individual origin of the speech system which we call language. *Bau*, in Humboldt's terminology should never be confused with the concept of an abstract, objective structure since the term *structure* in the sciences and in the social sciences at the end of the nineteenth century (and increasingly in post-war *structuralist* thought) came to be associated with a mechanical form of organisation which is imposed upon man without his acting upon the process.

But what did Humboldt mean by *Form*? Humboldt suggests that *Form* is the part of language which, through the activity or labour of the mind, has been *formed* into constant and *uniform* patterns of thinking and speaking: He gives the following definition:

> The constant and uniform [*gleichförmige*] element in this mental labour of elevating articulated sound to an expression of thought, when viewed in its fullest possible comprehension and systematically presented, constitutes the *form* of language [*die Form der Sprache*]. (1999: 50; 2003: 316)

This definition of *Form* requires further explanation, but before this is given, it is important to understand how *Form* is forged through the labour of the mind.

CHAPTER 9

The Work of the Mind

For Humboldt the division of a language into words and rules to be classified is a procedure that can be misleading. He believes this to be a scientific endeavour and it is one he engages in himself, but he is careful to delineate the boundaries of a scientific understanding of language when he says: 'The break-up into words and rules is only a dead makeshift of scientific analysis' (1999: 49). If this is so, it is because science can only ever analyse parts of language in isolation, abstracted from the context in which speech is uttered. This blinds science to what is most fundamental in language for Humboldt; the mind's creation of meaningful speech. In a similar way, a hundred years later, Whorf would stress that meaning is always at the heart of language and should consequently form the principle concern in the linguist's endeavour. For Humboldt, meaning arises in discourse from mental work, or what Heath calls *a work of the spirit*, in his translation of *eine Arbeit des Geistes* (Humboldt 1999: 49; 2003: 315).

Heath's translation echoes expressions made famous by the English philosopher John Locke (1632–1704); 'the workmanship of the mind' (1964: 279) and 'the workmanship of understanding' (281). And this is not inappropriate: Humboldt's model of language bears traces of Locke's model of understanding on four significant points:

1. Locke knew that words and concepts were not restricted to real objects to be found in the world around us. Many concepts (such

as fratricide and patricide, for example) show the activity of the mind in coupling concepts to facilitate understanding and communication. He referred to such couplings as 'mixed modes'.

2. Locke realised that such concepts differed from language to language and argued that the existence of untranslatable words was proof of this fact:

> A moderate skill in different languages will easily satisfy one of the truth of this, it being so obvious to observe great store of words [*sic*] in one language which have not any that answer them in another. Which plainly shows those of one country, by their customs and manner of life, have found occasion to make several complex ideas, and given names to them, which others never collected into specific ideas. This could not have happened if these species were the steady workmanship of nature, and not collections made and abstracted by the mind. (Locke 1964: 279–80)

3. Locke reasoned that the patterns which grew from and around central concepts in each language differed greatly: thus, *hour* in English and *hora* in Latin gave rise to concepts and expressions which were in no way comparable (280).

4. At a more fundamental level, Locke maintained that what seem to us at first sight to be the logical organising categories of nature herself 'appear, upon a more wary survey, to be nothing else but the artifice of understanding' (ibid.).

But if we are to understand Locke, it is important to grasp what he meant by 'artifice'. This term held none of the pejorative connotations often attributed to it in postmodernist critiques of language which denounce or celebrate polysemy and ambiguity as symptoms of the impossibility of establishing the meaning of a text. *Artifice* refers to the creative activity of the mind which fashions for itself concepts in order to enhance and widen understanding. Artifice builds bridges between man and the world by deepening his understanding of his world, as it builds bridges between man and man by furthering man's capacity for the expression and reception of ideas. By stressing man's role in creating the concepts and frameworks of language, and by stressing that man's creations differed from language to language, both Locke and Humboldt were leaving behind them a philosophical heritage that Trabant has called 'the Aristotelian tradition', a tradition which conceives of words as arbitrary signifiers designating things in objective reality, labels attached to objects. This tradition ran from Aristotle himself throughout the Middle Ages, and survived the death of Latin and the rise of national languages. Indeed the defenders of national languages ironically each affirmed that his own language was the equal of Latin, thus ironically championing the theory of the arbitrary nature of the linguistic sign (Trabant 1999). In contrast to this ancient and vigorous model, language was not conceived of by either Locke or Humboldt as an arbitrary reflection of the world around us. It was not the *witness* of thought, as Descartes described it (Trabant 1999: 15) or the *mirror of the human mind* as it was presented in Leibniz's model (Trabant 1999: 17). Just as language gives expression to man, Humboldt believed that language is itself the dynamic synthesis of man's expression.

The stress on 'work' (*Arbeit*) is characteristic of Humboldt's dynamic conception of language as an activity, or rather *interactivity*. Speech is doubly interactive since it entails not only subjects interacting with each other: it also implies an interaction between the mind and the concepts of the world which language furnishes the mind with. Humboldt understands linguistic activity in terms of energy. And he explains that human energy has three stages for him:

1. simply observing and gathering together impressions,
2. drawing ideas from this observation and this process of collecting,
3. assimilating ideas (Hansen-Løve 1972: 22).

This tripartite definition of energy opens the way to Humboldt's concept of *Bildung*, a term which is usually translated as, 'education', 'cultivation' or 'formation' and which implies the ongoing development of culture. What intrigued Humboldt was the tripartite relationship that existed between the mind, language and *Building* (the ongoing adventure of a nation's cultivation). Culture is clearly conceived by Humboldt as the *cultivation* and the development of man. But man will be doubly defined as both Man, the representative of humanity, and man in his individual being. These

two are never separated by Humboldt. Man as an individual cultivates himself within the realisation of humanity's development as
a whole. This sets Humboldt in an entirely different dimension to
the twentieth-century Western conception of culture and creativity
in which the artist stands outside society. While counter-culture
critics tend to see art or literature as working against society and
conventions, Humboldt situates culture at the centre of a society's
(or rather a nation's) development when he considers culture to be
the cultivation of the mind though language and thought.

This process of cultivation involves three interactive forces: the
cultivation of one's self, the cultivation of the mind of humanity,
and the cultivation of one's language. Since language is the organ of
thought, it does not simply reflect advances in thought, it manifests
them or bodies them forth; it gives *form* to them. And since neither
language nor the mind exists alone in abstraction, it is only through
the work of individual minds that culture and advancement in
thinking and in language are ever realised.

Clearly, the work of the individual mind is involved in any
reflection upon experience. But the activity of the mind is not
restricted to reflecting upon experience derived from the world.
If this were Humboldt's belief, he would be relying on the model
of perception left to us by the Enlightenment; that of perception
as a passive process. This is the model of perception adopted by
Boas and Sapir and, in as much as Whorf views man as inheriting
the language and the thought world he lives within, his view of
perception remains passive. But, as always, Humboldt conceives
the work of the mind as an activity, not a passive process of assimilating already-organised details. Language and the mind can both
be said to organise experience. Man makes distinctions between
things, thrusting his subjective concept outside of himself into the
world by virtue of the sonorous word which he shares with others.
This objectifies the subjective concept. Over time, this activity of
objectification of the subjective experience of thought comes to
settle into formed concepts and distinctions which will be passed
on to others as language develops. Therefore, the mind's organising
activity can be said to parallel the activity of language as it organises
concepts. Language's activity is an ongoing, assimilative activity,
however: it is only after the work of centuries that its effects become

constant and uniform. The parallel process, the mind's organisation of concepts of the world, on the other hand, takes place during the moment the individual strives to express himself.

Humboldt's conception of perception has its roots in Kant's faculty of understanding. Langham Brown has expressed doubts concerning the view that Humboldt's philosophy of language was derived from Kant as certain thinkers have suggested (Cassirer, Haym, Steinthal et al.), but he does nevertheless agree that both Humboldt and Kant were reacting against the model of perception shared by both French Rationalists and British Empiricists:

> Since for the British Empiricists knowledge consisted merely of the impressions left by the stream of sensations impinging on the *tabula rasa* of the mind, and thought merely of the combination and comparison of such impressions, perception was seen as a purely passive affair. The grouping of sensations by the individual came about solely through their spatial or temporal contiguity, and definitely not by any active imposition of groupings by the mind on the exterior flux of things. Just as knowledge was in this way a matter of single or multiple atomic sensations, so words were merely the labels attached to these single or multiple sensations after they had impinged. Language, according to such theories, did not play any part in deciding how the sensations were grouped, and far less did it play any part in determining what sensations were allowed to impinge in the first place. Just as in the contract theory of the origin of language adhered to equally by the British Empiricists and the French Rationalists language was considered to have arisen after the emergence of society and Reason, so in their epistemological theories it played no important part, but was merely a means of transmitting knowledge that had already been acquired. (Langham Brown 1967: 87)

In contrast to passive perception, Kant proposed his theory of the subjective conditions of judgement: in this theory, what had been conceived as perception was divided into two activities, *sensibility* and *understanding*. Sensibility, for Kant, deals with intuitions (*Anschaungen*) which involve sensory states which were taken to be the only basis of knowledge by the Empiricists. But to this Kant added the faculty for forming concepts, and since concepts have to be applied in judgements, it must follow that understanding, unlike sensibility, is active. One contemporary commentator, Scruton, summarises Kant's objection to the passive view of perception in the following terms:

> It is an assumption of empiricism that all concepts are derived from, or in some manner reducible to, the sensory intuitions which warrant their application. There can be no concept without the corresponding sensory stimulus, and it is in terms of such stimulus that the meaning of a concept must be given. Kant argued that this assumption was absurd. (Scruton 1996: 26)

Kant considered experience to be a species of knowledge and, as such, he held that it involved understanding. But understanding, for him, was rule-bound, and the rules, he felt forced to conclude, must exist within himself (the subject of experience) before objects could be presented to his faculty of understanding. These rules found expression in *a priori* concepts to which all objects of experience had to conform. Thus, perception, experience and understanding were bound up together and, at the centre of this whole complex experience, the subject was placed, actively perceiving, experiencing and understanding the world around him.

Certainly, much of this radically transformed concept of perception can be found in Humboldt's idea of the way we form concepts, and the development of that idea can indeed be traced back to Kant. But Langham Brown concludes:

> Humboldt was to replace the Kantian faculty of Understanding by language in his own version of epistemological theory; more specifically, languages came to be seen by Humboldt as the *a priori* frameworks of cognition.

The most important thing that Humboldt took from Kant was the argument that what is perceived is the result of an interaction between the human individual and the external world, between the subject and the object. What he added was, first, the notion that perception is structured by the active application of the framework of language to the flux of sensations, and, second, the idea that the frameworks of different languages differ. (Langham Brown 1967: 90)

As Langham Brown argues, for Humboldt, language is central to the process of perception (1967: 93). Language is the only means by which we can objectify the external world. But once more, language is conceived in terms of speech and speech retains its physical, oral-audible quality, as the expression and the reception of sound in spoken words. Ideas become fixed in language (and thus fixed in our shared thought) through their subjective expression in speech. Humboldt explained this in the following manner:

> Subjective activity fashions an *object* in thought. For no class of ideas can be regarded as a purely receptive contemplation of a thing already present. The activity of the senses must combine synthetically with the inner action of the mind, and from this combination the idea is ejected, becomes an object *vis-à-vis* the subjective power, and, perceived anew as such, returns back to the latter. But *language* is indispensable for this. For in that the mental striving breaks out through the lips in language, the product of that striving returns back to the speaker's ear. Thus the idea becomes transformed into real objectivity, without being deprived of subjectivity on that account. Only language can do this; and without this transformation, occurring constantly with the help of language even in silence, into an objectivity that returns to the subject, the act of concept-formation, and with it all true thinking, is impossible. (1999: 56)

It is not by chance that Humboldt uses the word *bildet*, when he claims that subjective activity *fashions* the object (as Heath translates it). *Bildet* brings us back to Humbolt's concept of culture and cultivation (*Bildung*). This becomes clear in the last few lines of the passage quoted above when Humboldt formulates his idea of the formation of concepts as *Bildung des Begriffs*. Language as the cultivation of the mind or spirit should be conceived, Humboldt believed, as the active building of concepts by individual minds which would fix these concepts by the act of speaking with others, and leave them embedded in the memory of men in speech handed down to subsequent generations. If there was a structure to language, then it was the objectified structure of these subjective gestures of thought formed in communicative speech. In this sense, *Bau* (structure), *bilden* as it was used to express the creative act of building, fashioning or moulding objects for our understanding, and *Bildung* (culture), were all three held to be inseparable in the ongoing development of language.

It would seem then that many of the things which understanding treats as real objects, such as time, love or courage, are in fact constructs of the mind (as Locke had already argued in his analysis of mixed modes). However, it would be misleading to suggest that what we consider as objects do not exist for Humboldt. Things do exist, as each of us can verify for himself. Tables, chairs, dogs and cats are endowed with real existence. In another (but very real) sense, love and courage exist for us: it makes sense to say that someone is 'brave' or 'full of love'. But Humboldt's point is that such constructs as chairs and dogs only exist for us in terms of objects and we can only speak of them as such by understanding them in terms of the concepts our language furnishes us with.

This may seem confusing if we consider the most everyday concepts and categories with which we are familiar. Let's consider, for example, dogs and cats: *cat* and *dog* are for us wholly different animals. Indeed their differences can be clearly defined and theories of evolution can advance facts about these differences. But though there is nothing epistemologically arbitrary about the distinction, it becomes clear that dogs and cats are concepts when we compare a Poodle with a Doberman. We could easily have chosen to formulate two generic categories in the canine species to separate the two, just as we have chosen, on concrete evidence to make a meaningful distinction between dogs and cats (which both belong to the genus, mammals). It is easy to imagine a language which would find our distinction between a cello and a violin difficult to grasp: indeed many people confuse the two instruments in English. This shows to what extent the refinement of our conceptual frameworks allows us to make distinctions among the things that surround us.

A table might seem a concept which designates a clearly defined object of experience which exists in and of itself independent of our understanding. But the essence of a table is not proper to the individual table. The table at which I am writing this is made of white Formica and metal, but none of these properties (whiteness, Formica, or metal) belong to our concept of tables. Though many tables are made of wood, neither is wood a property of tables, as my own table proves. This was plain to Locke who would have considered *table* to be a general idea, one of our 'creatures of understanding,' made by understanding for its own use (Locke 1964: 267). If all tables can be grouped together (and they can in a meaningful way, as English proves) then the signification that *table* has for us is nonetheless constructed by the mind of man and applied to all tables by him to aid him to communicate.

This becomes clear when we compare the ways different languages divide things up into objects for the faculty of understanding in its linguistic community. Langham Brown is right to remind us in the quotation above that, for Humboldt, the frameworks of different languages differ in terms of the concepts they have developed. *Table* seems to defy this: and in German, *der Tisch*, in French, *la table*, and in Czech *stůl* seem to refer to identical concepts in our understanding. But not so *chair*. Czech distinguishes between two wholly different concepts with the words *židle* and *křeslo*: the first referring to the kind of chair you might find at a table or in a classroom, the second referring to an armchair. The distinction between *chair* and *armchair* can be made in English of course, but the latter is conceived as a species of the genus *chair*, while in Czech two separate categories of understanding shape the distinction. French follows the same path in distinguishing between *chaise* (chair) and *fauteuil* (armchair).

Likewise, it becomes clear that words in different languages *contain* different concepts when we compare them. In French *sonnette*, *sonnnerie*, *cloche* and *clochette* are all considered as *bells* in English whether they are found at a door, resound at the school break, or hang from church towers or from the necks of cows and goats. Conversely, the French content themselves with *bord* for designating what we would term as *side*, *edge*, *shore*, or *rim*, depending upon whether we were referring to the side of a bed, a cliff, a sea, or a cup. Occasionally, linguists and translators will point to such variations in semantic categories and claim that they reflect the richness of one language and its superiority over the other, but to do this is spurious and the arguments advanced are often contradictory: at times a language will be held to be rich because of the variety of terms it employs, at other times a term will be held to be rich because of the multiple meanings a single word can evoke.

What these varying modes of conceptual categorisation did prove for Humboldt, however, was that:

> The mutual interdependence of thought and word illuminates clearly the truth that languages are not really means for representing already known truths, but are rather instruments for discovering previously unrecognised ones. The differences between languages are not those of sounds and signs but those of differing *worldviews* . . . objective truth always rises from the entire energy of subjective individuality. (Humboldt quoted by Langham Brown 1967: 94, my italics)

Humboldt argued that 'man surrounds himself in a world of sounds in order to take into himself a world of objects and operate upon them' (Langham Brown 1967: 95). This might seem to justify Hansen-Løve's conclusion that: 'It is language that constitutes the world and not the reverse' (*C'est le langage qui constitue le monde et non l'inverse*, Hansen-Løve 1972: 35: mT). But as with many such pithy aphoristic inversions, this one can be misleading. In denying that language is drawn from experience and by stressing the importance of language for categorising and framing experience, Hansen-Løve does not distinguish clearly between what we are designating as the real external world and our conception of that world. The former exists independent of ourselves, the latter is the formulation which our understanding through language has negotiated with the world.

Trabant expresses this relationship more accurately when he claims 'the world is given to us only through language' ('*le monde ne nous est donné qu'à travers le langage*', 1999: 58, mT). In his formulation, the world is taken to mean the world as we receive it. But since philosophers are often wary of existentialist denials of the world and playful postmodernist assertions concerning the relativity of experience which are based on the relativity of language, we should be wary of adopting Trabant's expression because the real world can, of course, impinge upon my experience in a non-linguistic fashion. I do not need a concept of a bus to be knocked over by one. Real things do exist, of course: language merely serves to organise them as objects for our understanding. Humboldt does not argue that the world only exists because we can speak about it. If we surround ourselves in a conceptual world of objects it is, he argues, because we seek to act in the world by acting upon the world of things as we have learned to understand them. If we were unable to act upon the things of the world, our concepts for them would be useless and would no doubt be abandoned (if they could ever have come into existence). To take a very concrete example, the mechanic's terminology of mechanical parts and their designated functions allows him to understand and repair your car.

Relativism, in the linguistic sense, as it is conceived of by Humboldt and defended by Langham Brown in his *Wilhelm von Humboldt's Conception of Linguistic Relativity*, does not imply a denial of reality or truth in the world around us: it simply affirms that our attempts to understand that world are language-bound. Mental activity works upon language which itself is only ever the distillation of mental activity manifested in language by thinking men and women speaking to one another. And different languages reflect the different courses and trajectories taken by the minds of men and women as they have sorted out the world of things and experiences into objects of their understanding in order to work in and with the world they find themselves in.

CHAPTER 10

Form

Mental activity, the work of the spirit, forms language, and because 'the existence of spirit as such can be thought of only in and as activity' (Humboldt 1999: 49), it follows that language is constantly being fashioned and refashioned. Linguistic study obliges us to dismember the structure (*Bau*) of languages, though Humboldt reminds us that this dissection should not delude us into thinking that we have touched the essential core of a language when we manage to speak of its grammar and its structure. Humboldt suggests that linguistic study should rather view each language as 'a *procedure* advancing by specific means to specific goals, and to that extent really to view them [languages] as *fashioned* by nations' (1999: 49). Once more, the word *fashioned* translates (in Heath's version) a key term for Humboldt. Humboldt expresses this idea as the *Bildungen der Nationen* (the cultivation of nations, or, rather, the cultivation *by* nations).

The cultivation of the nation is advanced by the cultivation of individual concepts by individual men and women. Here, nation is defined not in the nationalistic terms it has come to be associated with since the Second World War and the rise of fascism, but quite simply as *a body of people marked off by common descent, language, culture, or historical tradition.* What is often considered in terms of a power relationship between man and society, is conceived by Humboldt in terms of a dynamic interaction among men and women which culminates in generating a nation. Whenever we turn to language, we are confronted with its historical dimension: language is a creative process which has formed over time and which continues to form and reform itself.

> [. . .] in our study of language we find ourselves plunged throughout – if I may so put it – into a historical milieu, and [. . .] neither a nation nor a language among those known to us, can be called *original* [*ursprünglich*]. Since each has already received from earlier generations material from a prehistory unknown to us, the mental activity, which [. . .] produces the expression of thought, is always directed at once upon something already *given* [*Gegebenes*]; it is not a purely creative but a reshaping activity [*umgestaltend*]. (Humboldt 1999: 49–50, with German terms added by me from Humboldt 2003: 316)

Just as *Gestalt* has psychological associations in its modern usage, so the term used by Humboldt to express the idea that language is reshaped, *umgestaltend*, also indicates that this shaping and reshaping process comes about through mental activity. While the great thrust of linguistics in Germany at Humboldt's time and throughout the nineteenth century sought to penetrate the diachronic origin of language by tracing individual languages back to one ultimate *Ursprache*, Humboldt tackles the question of origin differently. He takes his bearings from speech which he considers to be the ongoing invention of language. Trabant (1999: 27) explains this as the influence of the philosophies of both Leibniz and Kant. In the linguistic philosophy that Humboldt is developing, speech, far from occupying the commonplace status often attributed to everyday communication, is elevated to a transcendental plane. Speech becomes the 'permanent genesis' of language (Trabant: ibid.). And the aim of linguistics should consequently be conceived of as the struggle to grasp and define the varying expressions of this permanent genesis, the ongoing reanimation of speech.

Nevertheless, we should be wary of taking this model for an explanation of the origin of language, because, as Humboldt points out above, the origin of language always escapes us. The course of a language, shaped by a nation, is never charted from the launching of its adventure, since languages always build upon previously formed languages, and none, so far as we can tell, have sprung up by themselves. The truism that nothing will come from nothing seems particularly apt when we study language. One obvious example would be the fashioning and refashioning of Romance languages which have their roots in Latin and which have been coloured by the tones of both the languages Latin transformed or displaced and other European languages which have exerted their influence on them since their formation. Take the dynamic distillation of Modern English from a mixture of Germanic tongues with French and Latin which added their own reshaping activity to Germanic syntax, grammar and rules of word-formation. What becomes uniform and constant from this dynamic synthesis can be termed the form of a language. This constancy is in no way fixed in stasis. On the contrary, something becomes and remains fixed in language because it is repeated again and again in the patterns of speech. Constancy in the form of language is not pinned down and prevented from moving: rather it is the continuing movement (or moving) of language along patterns provided by previous generations which maintains this constancy. This view of form was best described by one of our American linguists as the *grooves* along which speech moves in Sapir's analogy.

While form, for Humboldt was 'partly *fixed* and partly fluid' (1999: 62), twentieth-century grammars have tended to strive to define the unchanging model of grammar as a fixed form. In France at least, this quest has been fuelled not only by the abstract scientific aspirations of linguistics but also by the deeply embedded notion of the French language as a perfected cultural artefact which should, some argue, be protected. The object of adoration that the *Académie française* has made of French has, however, very little to do with the model Humboldt provides of language as an ongoing process which reshapes speech by virtue of the mental activity of individual speakers. In the same way, Humboldt warns us against a model of form 'as an abstraction fashioned by science' (1999: 50):

> [. . .] it would be quite wrong to see it [form] also in itself as a mere non–existent thought-entity of this kind. In actuality, rather, it is the quite individual *urge* whereby a nation gives

validity to thought and feeling in language. Only because we are never allowed to view this urge in the undivided totality of its striving, but merely in its particular effects on each occasion, are we also left with no recourse but to summarize the uniformity of its action in a dead general concept. In itself this urge is single and alive. (ibid.)

What we conceive of as grammar is, then, the overall impression we derive from multiple individual instances of speech. The form which is generated throughout these instances is one of a living urge towards the expression of thought. Our concept of form should therefore take this individual urge [*individueller Drang*] into account.

However, describing this individual and living urge towards expression proves to be highly problematical for the linguist. Because, though we do indeed gain a 'total impression of language' (*Gesamteindruck der Sprache*, 2003: 316), we fail to pin this impression down and clarify it in specific concepts. Should we abandon the definition of form that Humboldt is proposing then? Humboldt argues that we should not: we should, notwithstanding, launch ourselves into the study of the details of language because, he claims, 'The characteristic form of languages depends on every *single* one of their smallest *elements*; however inexplicable it may be in detail, each is in some way determined by that form' (1999: 50). We react to each detail by discerning a distinctness which is proper to each language. This leads Humboldt towards his idea that each language possesses something in its form which might be described as a *character*:

> The most distinct *individuality* plainly strikes the eye and is borne inexorably in our feeling. Languages, in this respect, can least inaccurately be compared with *human countenances* [*mit menschlichen Gesichtsbildungen*]. (ibid.)

Thus, for Humboldt, the true vocation of the linguist becomes the uncovering of this elusive form of language which animates individual exchanges in speech; an inner impulse which is ever oscillating between internalisation by the speaker and externalisation in his speech with others. He goes on to define this notion of form as both factual and individual:

The concept of form does not [. . .] exclude anything factual and individual; everything to be actually established on historical grounds only, together with the most individual features, is in fact comprehended and included in this concept. (1999: 52)

This confirms Humboldt in his conviction that we must proceed with the examination of details: but this is doubly frustrating, since not only is this a laborious process, it is also doomed to be incomplete. It is, ironically, exhausting but not exhaustive, since, as Humboldt points out:

> However much in it [language] we may fix and embody, dismember and dissect, there always remains something unknown left over in it, and precisely this which escapes treatment is that wherein the unity and breath of a living thing resides. (1999: 51)

Linguistic study is always then bafflingly fragmentary in its findings. Since the distinctions we are accustomed to drawing between grammar and vocabulary can never lead us to the true form of language as Humboldt understands it, scientific study should not be allowed to seduce us into a complacency derived from the clarity of the concepts which a scientific discipline is capable of generating. Such concepts are ultimately only of use for learning a language, Humboldt claims (ibid.). But the nature of a language which is expressed in its form goes far beyond these distinctions:

> The concept of the form of languages extends far beyond the rules of *word-order* and even beyond those of *word-formation*, insofar as we mean by these the application of certain logical categories, of active and passive, substance, attribute, etc. to the roots of basic words. It is peculiarly applicable to the formation of the *basic words* themselves, and must in fact be applied to them as much as possible, if the nature of the language is to be truly recognizable. (ibid.)

The study of language as a human faculty was always held by Humboldt to be inseparable from the study of languages (a fact which sets him apart from much twentieth century linguistic study). His aim was to compare languages in order to trace each of their individual trajectories as expressions of a nation's spirit:

> Through exhibiting the form we must perceive the specific course which the language, and with it the nation it belongs to, has hit upon for the *expression of thought*. We must be able to see how it relates to *other languages*, not only in the particular goals prescribed to it, but also in its reverse effect upon the mental activity of the nation. (1999: 52)

Thus the study of individual speech and the individual parts of speech were harnessed together in a project that was, Humboldt hoped, to lead us towards an (albeit incomplete) explanation of the trajectory of both a nation and its language and the reciprocal influence of the two in the formation of one another. From the scattered impressions of individual speech, we are asked to try to work our way back to that overwhelming impression of the individuality of each language:

> The same unity must therefore be found again in the description; and only if we ascend from the scattered elements to this unity do we truly obtain a conception of the language, since without such a procedure we are manifestly in danger of not even understanding the said elements in their true individuality, and still less in their real connection. (ibid.)

This warning is particularly pertinent in the study of the relationship between worldview and language: for since the character of a language can only be discerned in the living force of its form – its shaping and reshaping of concepts in speech – and since this form can only be understood after the rigorous analysis of details, any opinion advanced about the character of nations and the worldviews of languages which is not based upon a rigorous knowledge of a language will be unfounded: ultimately it will have no more penetrating force than the fanciful imaginings of an unfocused mind. Humboldt's project is admittedly daunting in its scope and ambitious in its aims, but if it is impressionistic it is impressionistic in its attempt to rigorously hold together our view of the whole while ascertaining the exact role of the detail, the part, within that whole.

The impressionistic musings of the French cultural thinker Stamm (and even of Whorf at times) are of an entirely different order. The former starts out with the romantic cliché that African cultures are spiritual and full of ancient wisdom, then tries to gather evidence to support this idea. Whorf's quest is to represent his impression of the metaphysical worldview of a language by analysing its grammar. But neither Whorf nor Stamm speak the languages they study fluently. Consequently, their impressions are not nourished by the rich resonance that comes from interacting meaningfully with speakers of the languages themselves. For the native speaker, any word takes on a rich and varied meaning as it is used at work, in the street and at home, or as it is rediscovered in various contexts in films and books. Words for the language student, on the other hand, remain to a large extent items on vocabulary lists, and each term is invariably translated back into an equivalent term in the student's native tongue up until the point at which he or she masters the foreign language sufficiently to perceive that a vast number of terms do not, in fact, coincide in the two languages. Until this stage is reached, writers and thinkers often find themselves incapable of wading out from the shore of their own language, conceptually speaking, to swim off to foreign shores. While Stamm allows a Western perspective to condition her vision of African worldviews and Whorf seeks to find deeper meaning in form, Humboldt advocates that we seek always to listen to the meaning that men express in their spoken and written words.

CHAPTER 11

Creativity, Culture and Character

As the friend of Schiller, Humboldt was influenced by the *Storm and Stress* pre-Romantic movement (*Sturm und Drang*) to which both Schiller and Goethe belonged. During the 1790s, Humboldt was engaged in working on Goethe's epic poem, *Hermann and Dorothy*. It is not by chance then that the metaphors which structure Humboldt's thought and the vocabulary that colours it are often reshaped from the words, concepts and metaphors common to the discourse of the Zeitgeist that Goethe and Schiller incarnated. Humboldt incessantly returns to formulations of an organic and sexual kind to describe the growth of languages as a process of fertilization and gestation. And, as we have seen above, the speaking subject is characterised as being animated by a vital inner urge to break through to expression in much the same way as the lyrical personae of Goethe's poems strive to express themselves. The expression *individueller Drang* (individual urge) is not, it would seem, accidental.

Humboldt was no doubt in agreement with Goethe when he argued that the German of the eighteenth century had been going through a period of cultural, intellectual and linguistic gestation. He may well have agreed with Goethe on the poet's estimation of his own contribution to the advancement of German culture. Goethe, for his part, described the German of his youth as 'a clean tablet, on which one could hope to paint good things with pleasure' (Goethe, in Eckermann 1998: 295). And though the great poet expressed some doubts about the contribution of the Romantics of the first decades of the nineteenth century (ibid.), he saw the gestation of German culture as an ongoing process into which he had been born and which he had helped nurture. This process of cultivation, this great project, was, in his opinion, far from complete. As far as the average German was concerned, Goethe believed:

> We [Germans] have indeed been properly cultivated for a century; but a few centuries more must elapse before so much mind and elevated culture will become universal amongst our people that they will appreciate beauty like the Greeks, will be inspired by a beautiful song; before it will be said of them, 'it is long since they were barbarians'. (Goethe, in Eckermann 1988: 202)

For Germans of Goethe's generation and the generation that came after him (to which Humboldt belonged), literature formed an essential part of the project for cultivating the German spirit. It is easy to see how such an idea of the role of literature could have flattered the ego of a writer. Yet though Goethe is sometimes portrayed as a self-satisfied promoter of his own Genius-cult, he was surprisingly modest when he compared the paltry success of his own folk poems with those of the Scottish poet, Burns. While he said of his own poems that 'among the *people* they have no sound' (ibid.), those of Burns lived in the mouth of the people (*im Munde des Volkes lebten*, Goethe, in Eckermann 1982: 542):

> Now take up Burns. How is he great, except through the circumstance that all the songs of his predecessors lived in the mouth of the people – that they were, so to speak, sung at his cradle; that, as a boy, he grew up amongst them, and the high excellence of these models so pervaded him that he had therein a living basis on which he could proceed further? Again, why is he great, but from this: his own songs at once found susceptible ears amongst his compatriots; sung by reapers and sheaf-binders, they at once greeted him in the field; and his boon-companions sang them to welcome him at

the ale-house? *That* surely was the way something could be done. (in Eckermann 1998: 202)

Here we have some of the important elements which went to create Humboldt's theory of the importance of literature for a people's language. Though he was convinced that language should be studied in terms of the expression of the speaking man, he considered literary texts and texts in general to be fundamental records of the individual expression of the human mind's activity in language. Poets and philosophers worked with the linguistic frameworks or the form of language that they inherited, but their own writing extended that form and those frameworks as they refashioned the language to a greater degree than the average man did (though the average man nonetheless sustained or reshaped his language to some extent). Humboldt expressed this in the following terms:

> This is a continuing harvest from the *literature* of the people, though especially there from its *poetry* and *philosophy*. The extension of the other sciences does more to furnish language with a single material, or divides and defines the existing matter with greater fixity; but poetry and philosophy make contact, in a wholly different sense, with the innermost in man himself, and thus also have a stronger and more formative effect upon the language so intimately entwined with his nature. (1999: 87)

Humboldt felt that the importance of the poet and the philosopher lay in the fact that they distilled the language: as writers they gave it to their fellow natives to drink. For Goethe, Burns refashioned the ballads he learned in his cradle and brought them back to life with the inspiration of his genius. Humboldt could well have been thinking about the transformation of German culture and of Goethe himself when he evoked the importance of a golden age of literature for the development of a language:

> Those languages, therefore, in which, at least in one epoch, a poetic and philosophical spirit has been dominant, are also the most capable of *perfection* in their *progress*; and doubly so, if

this dominance has sprung from a spontaneous impulse, and has not been aped from abroad. (ibid.)

The perfection of languages in their progress (*Vollendung in ihrem Fortgange*, 2003: 353–4) clearly implies that for Humboldt, there is something teleological in the development of languages. But the progress of languages cannot be compared with the Enlightenment model of progress towards one fixed shared goal with the achievement of which universal man is supposed to find his realisation. Languages were following different paths in Humboldt's opinion, or, to use an organic metaphor that Humboldt might have appreciated, languages were reaching out like different branches of human consciousness. Nevertheless, in Humboldt's conception of the perfection of language, there is none of the relativism that we might be inclined to expect from a writer like Stamm or the defenders of ecolinguistics.

Language can be considered as a form of project which moves within the scope of its own individual emotional, intellectual and spiritual needs towards a greater refinement in its form of expression. Does this mean that the mind is free to express itself in speech? To some extent, this would seem to be the case. Since it is only through language that concepts come into existence for consciousness, language comes to be conceived by Humboldt as the mind's exploration of the conceptual freedom which it has itself created. Rather than the master–slave, subject–object conception of language in which either the mind controls the language or language controls the mind, Humboldt posits the idea of language as a free space which the mind opens up for itself.

Without language, reflection upon objects, as concepts of the mind, would be impossible. This is because the object for the mind does not exist in Humboldt's opinion other than via the conceptualisation of experience that has taken place and continues throughout all speech (1999: 59). Humboldt inevitably implies that there are limits to language, but his version of linguistic limits does not, however, imprison the individual in a language which is alien to him. Humboldt might have accepted that the collective distillation of usage has opened up paths or *grooves* to the mind (as Sapir expressed it), but he would not have concurred with Whorf's seeming impatience with these patterns, or *ruts*, as the latter called them. On the contrary Humboldt argues:

> [. . .] the whole mode of *perceiving* things *subjectively* necessarily passes over into cultivation and the use of language. For the *word* arises from this very perceiving; it is a copy, not of the object itself, but of the image thereof produced in consciousness. Since all objective perception is inevitably tinged with *subjectivity*, we may consider every individual, even apart from language, as a unique aspect of the world-view. (ibid.)

Linguistic symbols and signs exert no tyranny over the individual because each one of us has our own subjective notion of what that sign means within the interactive semantic euphony of language echoing within ourselves. When we speak, we both explore the paths that language provides for us and break out on new paths of our own.

While Whorf dreamt of escaping the confines of Standard Average European by breaking into the exotic frameworks of alternative worldviews, Humboldt, however much he might have enjoyed the same mind-opening experience of language-learning, felt, nevertheless, that freedom could be found within writing, speech and within the very form of language itself. Speech deprived of subjective freedom is unthinkable for Humboldt. Languages themselves require freedom in his opinion in order to form themselves because it is by freely linking things through language that the mind finds expression for its ideas. This concept of freedom in Humboldt's work involves the constant linking of sounds to concepts in order to further define them and their relations to one another.

Humboldt is not simply thinking of an allegorical or abstract idea of building here: he is picturing the physical reality by which speech is generated. Humboldt was making an affirmation that Lakoff and Johnson (1999) were to make almost two hundred years later with their claim that 'philosophy is in the flesh', when he explained that the mediation between sound and concept was always of a sensory character. Concepts are derived from concrete physical terms. Humboldt gives the example of the term *Vernunft* (reason) which contains and is derived from the term *nehmen* (to take). He also offers the term *Verstand* (understanding) which likewise depends upon and evokes *stehen* (to stand) (Humboldt 1999: 92). Our own term *understanding* mirrors this link between comprehension and stance.

If language needs freedom, then it needs it in order to give its creative impulse free reign to extend the range of these semantic and sonorous links to further elaborate our capacity for expression. *Sonorous* is a word that implies literary rather than linguistic connotations for us today, but the principle of *euphony* was fundamental in Humboldt's opinion for all language use. Euphony could not be reduced to a formal quality: euphony was meaningful. However it was because euphony was also formal that the meaning resonated with greater force as the links forged between related concepts were sounded in the morphemes used to construct the words that bodied forth those concepts.

The pure principle of creativity in language, for Humboldt, generated semantic-sonorous links which gave an increasingly greater force and harmony to language. The purity of the form of a language was never realised to its fullest extent in any language in existence, as far as Humboldt knew. This was because languages always interact with one another and arbitrary word-forms are introduced which do not resonate within the language by echoing other related concepts. For example, our English word *connoisseur* derives from eighteenth-century French in which the verb 'to know' was *connoître* (not *connaître*, as it is in modern French). For the French of the time, *connoisseur* and *connoître* were linked logically by deriving *knower* from *to know*. This semantic and euphonic link has a parallel in present-day French in *connaisseur/connaître*. This logical link, the echo of an internal coherence, is lost to the English speaker. If the word *connoisseur* carries any connotations for the English-speaker then they are more likely to be of a cultural than a euphonic nature, since words borrowed from French from the seventeenth century onwards often tended to be of an uplifted, elegant or artistic nature.

The present-day borrowings from English face a similar fate. The prosaic, concrete words used to generate the terminology of IT in English are clearly visible in the terms *download*, *update*, *input* and *output*. But whether these terms are adopted by another language or translated, the words that enter that language no longer bear the trace of the modes by which the mind created them. This goes some way to explaining the hostility English meets with as it encroaches on other languages. Purists sometimes resent words which do not *fit into* the semantic networks and phonological sound system of their language. Linguistic purity is questionable as an ideal, and non-existent as a reality, however. No language springs up in and of itself. And, as any dictionary of etymology in any language will amply prove, no language has preserved itself from the intense and extensive influence of various languages. Nonetheless, Humboldt believed that Sanskrit reflected a very pure form of euphony, and this euphony, far from being a simple formal embellishment, was the harmony and unity created by the meaningful activity of the mind.

So does the mind become increasingly creative as language is extended and sounds and concepts further its euphony? Does the freedom of the mind increase with the refinement of language? Humboldt's answer to this is paradoxical. At the beginning of a language, Humboldt speculates (having admitted that no model is available for study), men 'struggle to express their thoughts, and this urge, together with the inspiring stimulus of success, engenders and sustains their creative power' (148). He likens this to the process of crystallisation in which one crystal builds upon another, though he is careful to remind us that language remains at all times 'the living creation of the mind' (ibid.). Once this process of crystallisation is fully completed, language becomes available for man's use as a 'finished product' or 'instrument' (*Werkzeug*). But it must be remembered that language should never be conceived as a product in objectified inanimate terms, in Humboldt's linguistic philosophy. Language offers itself up as an instrument for the work of the mind, and the mind comes to inhabit language through using it. 'Language is formed by speaking, and speaking is the expression of thought or feeling' (ibid.).

In one sense then, thinking becomes freer with the ongoing development of language which offers up an ever greater number of patterns and paths to follow in the accumulated thought-activity which has crystallized into speech. And yet, as these patterns and paths emerge, the desire for creative individual thinking wanes. We feel enticed to think along the same paths and patterns that others have formed for us within our language:

[. . .] the further a language has advanced in its grammatical structure, the fewer become the cases requiring a new decision. The struggle to express thought becomes weaker, therefore; the more the mind now employs what has already been created, the more its creative urge relaxes, and with that also its creative power. As against this, the mass of material produced in the edifice increases, and this external mass, now reacting upon the mind, imposes its own characteristic laws, and hampers the free and independent operation of the intelligence. (149)

To express this in Sapir's terms, as language traces increasingly perfect grooves, the temptation to break out of these grooves decreases. As temptation wanes, our actual creative intellectual power to innovate ebbs away. Like a muscle not regularly exercised, the creative impulse weakens.

Perfection in language becomes, therefore, the perfection of a utensil. Perfection is conceived more as an ongoing process by Humboldt, but we can gather from many passages in his work that there are stages in the development of languages, and different languages realise their different stages to a fuller or lesser degree. Humboldt makes it clear that the vocation of the poet and the vocation of the philosopher are to raise language to a higher state for the greater good of the nation. Literature has the power to reshape the average man's capacity to think, feel and speak: in Goethe's terms, to transform the barbarian into a civilised man.

Humboldt expressed himself in more nuanced terms. *Barbarians* is not a word he would have used, and he refused to accept that primitive languages existed (something which makes him a radical throughout nineteenth-century linguistics). The mumbling barbarian, grappling with the creation of basic concepts, was no longer available for study at the beginning of the nineteenth century: he belonged to the very distant past in Humboldt's opinion. But despite refusing to believe in primitive languages, Humboldt is far from according the same value to all languages. Each has its own character: this is a belief firmly anchored in Humboldt's thought, though the development or cultivation of that character can be realised to a fuller or lesser extent. And literature forms part of the development of this character:

Language develops its character primarily during the periods of its *literature*, and in the preparatory phase that leads to this. For it is then withdrawing more from the commonplaces of material life and raising itself to the pure evolution of thought and to free expression. (1999: 151)

The 'evolution of thought' (*Gendankenentwicklung*) and 'free expression' (*freie Darstellung*) mentioned here appear to come about in the work of minds which turn from the everyday usefulness of language reserved for the purposes of expression. But, in turning away, creative or literary thought does not reject the shared language of expression. This freer expression derives from the shared language of the nation which literature will serve by furthering the 'forming of the spirit' (ibid.), and it will further its spirit by making language an increasingly individualized mode of expression.

This is a very different model of language change from the one usually found in contemporary linguistics in which a community is represented as unthinkingly adopting (or being subjected to) a language shift. Language itself and language change are never imposed upon the individual as an external and impersonal force, Humboldt believes, since it is always the individual who reshapes language and refines it.

So long as the mind of the people is at work in living individuality [*lebendiger Eigenthümlichkeit*] within it, and upon its language, the latter receives the refinements and enrichments which in turn have a stimulating effect upon the mind. (1999: 150; 2003: 413)

Individual creativity refines and enriches the language we speak: and that refined and enriched language exerts a creative influence upon our minds as we spiral up in language towards a greater creativity.

If Humboldt extols the refining force of literature and celebrates the practical implications of literature's creativity for the refinement of the minds of those who speak the language, he is not, nevertheless, advocating that we honour for all time the literature that has helped to forge the spirit and character of a language. On the contrary, he suggests that in the development of a language, what was once fresh and new, vigorous and vital, must in time become worn out and insipid:

> [. . .] in the course of time, an epoch may ensue in which language, as it were, outgrows the mind, and the latter, in its own languor, having ceased to be self-creative [*selbstschöpferisch*], plays an increasingly empty game with idioms and forms of the language that originated from truly meaningful use. This, then, is a second *wearying* of language, if we consider the extinction of its external formative urge to be the first. In the second, the bloom of its character withers, though languages and nations can again be aroused and uplifted from this condition by the genius of particular great men. (1999: 150–1; 2003: 413)

Did Humboldt have Schiller and Goethe in mind when he spoke of the great men who could bring a language back to life, arouse it and uplift it from its weariness? Their examples as great individuals must surely have inspired Humboldt and shown him how a language can be transformed by literature.

The influence of the individual character of one writer upon the language leaves Humboldt with a problem which must be squared, however: if languages are each to be conceived as individual characters, as he suggests they might be (though he stresses this is only the least inaccurate way of expressing their individual forms), then how can the individual transform the language and make it his own by asserting his creative impulse as Goethe and Schiller might be said to have transformed German? How can a language which is supposed to have an individual character serve, furthermore, the multiplicity of tasks that are required of it by the diverse individuals of the nation to which it belongs? Humboldt poses this question in the following manner:

> It seems strange [. . .] that languages should be able to possess an individual character – apart from what is furnished by their outer organization – since each is destined to serve as a tool for the most varied individualities. For leaving aside differences

of sex and age, a nation surely embraces every nuance of human idiosyncrasy. (1999: 151)

In answer to this question, Humboldt replies that even when languages are used for similar tasks, they are used in a manner that is specific to each language and this means that they 'differ in their mode of apprehension and response' (ibid.).

> [. . .] this difference grows greater still with language, since it enters into the most secret recesses of the mind and temperament. Now everyone uses language to express his most particular individuality; for it always proceeds from the individual, and each uses it primarily for himself alone. Yet it suffices everyone, insofar as words, however inadequate, fulfil the urge to express one's innermost feelings. Nor can it be claimed that language, as a universal medium, reduces theses differences to a common level. It does indeed build bridges from one individuality to another, and is a means of mutual understanding; but in fact it enlarges the difference in itself, since by clarifying and refining concepts it produces a sharper awareness of how such difference is rooted in the original cast of mind. (ibid.)

The individuality of the language, far from being in contradiction with the idea that individuals use language differently, is itself further individualised by the activity of individuals.

> The possibility of serving to express such diverse individualities seems, therefore, to presuppose in language itself a perfect lack of character, with which it can by no means be reproached. It actually combines the two opposing properties of dividing itself, as one language in the same nation, into an infinity of parts, and as such an infinity, of uniting itself, as one language of a particular character, against those of other nations. (ibid.)

Language holds together an infinity of individualities within itself and this is the very force which furthers its individual character. This leads Humboldt to the following exclamation:

> How differently each man takes and uses the same mother-tongue, we find – if it were not already obvious in everyday life – on comparing major writers, each of whom creates his own idiom. But the difference of character among various languages, such as Sanscrit, Greek and Latin, for example, is apparent at first sight on comparing them. (ibid.)

Man, Humboldt argues, is always faced with a choice in the way he uses language. But this is not an either/or choice, it is a choice between three options. He 'couples *reality* to himself, as an object he accepts or a material he shapes or else makes his own way independently thereof' (158). In other terms, Humboldt is introducing a tripartite model for the way we adopt language when we speak.

1. He can adopt the words, concepts, patterns and modes of thought language offers him, unthinkingly accepting them as appropriate and adequate to his needs.
2. He realises they are the material with which he thinks and he proceeds to reshape them to his needs.
3. Alternatively, he can look for an entirely different form of expression and reject the solutions that the work of the mind has already *worked out* and offers him up for use or transformation.

These three options might be summarised as, *language use*, *language adaptation* and *language invention*.

Humboldt concludes: 'The original characteristic mark of man's individuality is the depth to which he strikes his roots into reality, and his manner of doing so' (ibid.). Literature is vital for language in that it offers one of the greatest expressions of individuality. Jürgen Trabant expresses this in terms of a 'violence' that the individual, speaker or writer, does 'to the power of language' when he reshapes it (Trabant 1992: 56). But while Trabant is justified in using this term, since he is quoting Humboldt himself, the term *violence* is, nevertheless misleading. Though literature has the power to trans-form language, this transformation has little in common with that call for a violent rebellion against the tyranny of the language which can be found in various modernist and postmodernist manifestos which gained currency in America and Europe in the inter-war and post-war periods (and of which the Dadaist movement is probably the most famous example).

Speech does not violate language, and the opposition between the individual and language (and especially between the poet and language – a commonplace one in twentieth-century Western aesthetics) would have struck Humboldt as a curious one. This is because creative poetic expression does not contradict the nature of language or the practice of speech. For Humboldt, the power of language is always individual. Language is an ongoing expression of individual urges. Speech always manifests the individual's will towards expression and it is only thanks to individuals and their urges that language can survive as a living expression of a group or nation. Change, far from attacking language, is thus one of its essential functions and properties.

Of all the writers and thinkers to have been influenced by the thought of Humboldt, the French thinker and translator, Henri Meschonnic (born 1932) is perhaps the one to show the greatest sensitivity to this point in Humboldt's thought. Taking on board Humboldt's idea of the subjective transformation of language and the importance of literature for language, Meschonnic has defended his theory of poetics in which the subject of the text creates himself as the speaking *I* by virtue of his discourse. The *I* of a poem, is not an individual for Meschonnic, but a subject of language, who comes into being and constructs himself within the poem. The individual exists, of course, but the linguistic subject (*le sujet du discours*), the *I*, only exists in language, in the act of speaking or writing. The highly individual or specific way the poet treats accents, sounds (in rhymes and alliteration), and the meaningful links he forges between words and his own personal way of organising those words, all form part of what Meschonnic describes as a heightened *subjectivation* of language.

Just as, in Humboldt's linguistic philosophy, language reveals the work of the mind that links up related concepts such as *standing* and *understanding*, so the writer, in Meschonnic's poetics, invents new meaningful subjective links between words. This can be illustrated by bringing Meschonnic's poetics to bear upon an example from Shakespeare. When Petruchio, the protagonist of *The Taming of the Shrew*, explains his reasons for coming to Padua, he expresses himself by rhyming the two key words of his sentence:

And I have thrust myself into this maze,
Haply to *wive* and *thrive* as best I may (I, ii, 244)

As Petruchio makes perfectly plain, wiving and thriving are for him inseparable. Not only will finding a wife assure his posterity, it will also (he hopes) consolidate his fortunes. The negotiations with his future father-in-law make his philosophy (or strategy) perfectly clear. In the lines above, Petruchio's thought and personality are bodied forth in the link between marriage and riches, and this link is highlighted by this sonorous coupling of words.

Standing and *understanding*, in Humboldt's example, are linked etymologically and no doubt that link came about by an analogical or metaphorical intuition which conceived of comprehension in terms of the ability to perceive, and in turn related perception logically to sight and viewpoint. In the Shakespearean example, on the other hand, it is sound, not logic or analogy which permits the harnessing of *wiving* and *thriving*. But what is crucial is that it is the individual intelligence of Shakespeare which forges a meaningful link between these two hitherto separate ideas. Once the link has been established, it resonates within the memory of speakers of a linguistic community, and can consequently shape their thought and pattern their expression in speech.

But literature is not only concerned with forging new links, it also offers an infinite number of examples of semantic links that can be unearthed. Shakespeare's characters in *The Taming of the Shrew* explore the way the concept of *bearing* has been formed in language. When Petruchio invites his harsh-tongued Katerina to sit on his knee, she replies:

Asses were made to bear and so were you.

To which Petruchio swiftly replies:

Women are made to bear, and so are you. (II, i, 247)

In this way, Peruchio plays with the double meaning of the word 'bearing'; to bear a burden and to bear children, just as Katerina had played on the double meaning of *ass* as a beast of burden and a term of abuse. Shakespeare offers particularly rich examples of the way a writer can unearth links between concepts and forge new links between ideas, but most literature will afford similar examples.

As Meschonnic knows very well though, this activity is not restricted to poetry or literature as a whole. Similar word-play can be found in jokes and advertising for example. *Subjectivication* is a fundamental part of language, an inalienable facet of its multiform nature. Without subjectivation language it would wither, lose its colour and its expressive potential for us. This is the lesson which poetry teaches to linguistics: that far from rebelling against language, poetry is a refinement of language's subjective potential, one means by which the individual can, to adopt Humboldt's expression, strike his roots into reality.

The way men make meaning with language was the crux of language study for Humboldt and the very thing that made language study crucial as a discipline among the humanities and the sciences. Humboldt admired linguists of his time like Franz Bopp (1791–1867), the German specialist of Sanskrit famous for having furthered the study of etymological links between the Indo-European languages, and Jacob Ludwig Carl Grimm (1785–1863) his compatriot, who published widely on grammar and lexicography, and who would write the famous German dictionary to which his name was given (besides collecting the fairy tales that were to become famous throughout Europe) with his brother Wilhelm Carl Grimm (1786–1859). Nonetheless, Humboldt's project differed from theirs fundamentally and the energy with which he advocated his project for comparing the worldviews of languages and the time he spent developing his concept of *Weltansicht* seem to testify to a feeling of impatience with the linguistics of his time. Humboldt would most probably have criticised the formalist linguistics with its scientific aspirations which was to develop throughout the nineteenth and twentieth centuries. The objectivist scientific approach certainly maintained the empirical research and analytical rigour that Humboldt praised and practised, but it failed on three accounts:

1. It stressed the importance of collecting and categorising fragmentary details without integrating them into a model of the language as a whole.

2. It stressed the study of form at the cost of almost wholly excluding the study of meaning.

3. By excluding the way men make meaning, it made language into an object of understanding rather than an activity to be studied as a subjective experience of reality.

Consequently, linguistics risked forcing the question of man out of the philosophy of language. In contrast to linguistics as a modern scientific endeavour, the empirically enlightened, linguistic anthropology that Humboldt was advocating placed man at the centre of all language study. This allowed Humboldt to formulate and to investigate questions which were to become increasingly marginalised in modern linguistics. Those questions concerned the study:

1. of the way language both reflects and moulds our experience of the world,

2. of the essentially creative origin and animating force of all speech,

3. of the way in which language forms the character of the nation, its worldview and in turn, the way in which this character-forming language is shaped by the creative intellectual efforts of speaking individuals.

The question which arises with Humboldt's definition of linguistic anthropology is: How do we gain entrance into the worldview of a foreign language? To put it in other terms: How do we catch its character? The difficulties which beset the attempt to answer this question will be discussed in the following three chapters.

CHAPTER 12

Catching the Character

The project that Humboldt was outlining at the time of his death for the study of the individual characters of nations and languages in all their kaleidoscopic variety is an exciting and daunting one. Who can hope to master the world's languages (or even a handful of them) to a degree of competence sufficient to allow him to compare them in any meaningful way? Even the question proves problematic. What do we mean by mastering a language? What do we mean by meaningfully comparing languages? The idea of mastering a language is usually reserved for foreigners and children who reach a certain stage of linguistic competence which is generally agreed to be acceptable. At this stage, the speaker is said to communicate meaningfully while respecting the grammar of the language. But does such a stage of linguistic competence allow the speaker to appreciate fully the worldview of the language?

Much comparative linguistics of the second half of the twentieth century was fuelled by the desire to *map* languages. Those who embarked upon the mapping of languages quite simply abandoned the search for meaning in language. Language was reduced to form (in the grammatical sense) and grammars were classified and catalogued. This attempt to map languages aimed only at what might be called a *formal understanding* of them. Formal understanding was something that Hegel criticised in the Enlightenment's project to establish scientific knowledge. Such understanding, Hegel argued, surveys the whole, but in doing so, it stands above the individual existence which it is talking about: i.e. it does not see it, but only labels it (Adorno 1991: 37).

Mapping can be considered a form of labelling. In mapping languages, language difference was seen as a problem of study, which once defined, was solved: the languages themselves, the speakers and what they spoke about could then be forgotten. Definition became a form of disposal. One might be justified in questioning whether the specialists who indulged in this project were actually interested in the languages they studied. For the linguists who sought to compare multiple languages often did not master the languages they studied to anything like the level that a child or a foreigner might be said to 'master English'. As a consequence, meaning and worldview were excluded from the comparative linguistics project and the comparison of languages became the juxtaposition and contrasting of formal grammars (which unlike lexis, pronunciation and syntax, can be *mastered*, or at least theoretically comprehended with relatively little study). The attempt to compare languages in such a way would probably have struck Humboldt as a curious pursuit engaged in by those who had forgotten the greater more fundamental meaning of language for each speaker within his own linguistic community. Indeed, language study which contents itself with the study of form as an end in itself is absurd and, quite literally, *meaningless*. What good can come from mapping territories we have not visited and do not wish to visit? Humboldt was a philologist (a lover of languages) and to him such comparative linguistics would no doubt have seemed like cartography for the sake of it.

The difference between Humboldt's project and recent attempts at formal comparisons in comparative linguistics cannot be overstressed. While Humboldt sought (probably in a similar manner to Whorf) to extend the horizons of his own consciousness by moving into the different worldviews that other languages offer, the project to map languages that we do not speak can only ever reveal to us the outlines of our own models. Though those outlines may correspond to something real within the make-up of other languages, they in no way reveal the inner richness of those languages or enlighten us as to what they have to offer us, i.e. another way of living, thinking and feeling.

Humboldt wished to catch something of the character of the worldview as it manifested itself in each language and as it orchestrated the sensitivity of thought and feeling of each speaker that inhabited that worldview. For him, the worldview (*Weltansicht*) resides in the language, and worldviews vary from language to language. A worldview is constituted in the language and experienced by the individual as a lived sensual experience. The sounds man makes and hears intervene between him and the world:

> As the individual sound stands between man and the object, so the entire language steps in between him and the nature that operates, both inwardly and outwardly, upon him. (1999: 60)

But though language intervenes between man and nature, this intervention should not be conceived in terms of a barrier. Language does not build a wall between man and the world. It links man to the world, by transforming his internal consciousness and allowing him to formulate the objects of the world within himself.

> He surrounds himself in a world of sounds, so as to take up and process within himself the world of objects. [. . .] Man lives primarily with objects, indeed, since feeling and acting in him depend on his presentations, he actually does so exclusively, as language presents them to him. (ibid.)

Humboldt understands the relationship between man and language as a two-way process in which language penetrates man and man penetrates language.

> By the same act whereby he spins language out of himself, he spins himself into it, and every language draws about the people that possesses it a circle whence it is possible to exit only by stepping over at once into the circle of another one. (ibid.)

In the other words, there is no outside to language. We can only step from within the circle of one language into another language, and taking that step takes us into another worldview.

For this reason, language does not *reflect* thought for Humboldt. We cannot extract any form of hermeneutic meaning from language and formulate it in an abstract, non-linguistic or supra-linguistic form. Conversely, we do not *put* meaning into form, as the expression *to put something into words* suggests. Language constitutes the circle of consciousness within which we think and within which our conceptual sensitivity has developed. We cannot therefore escape from the circle into a hermeneutic hinterland which can dispense with the faculty of language.

This is something that is revealed in the process of translation. The translator does not extract the meaning, then lay it to one side until he decides to invest it in the other language. Languages are more like stepping stones. It is only by juxtaposing words and expressions that the translator becomes able to identify similarities. Words can be defined in terms of foreign words just as they can be defined in terms of synonymous words within the same language. But they cannot be defined in terms of any abstract non-linguistic criteria. Only by firmly placing his foot upon the concepts of the target language, can the translator transmit meaning from one thought to another. To take up the stepping stones analogy once more, the translator, stepping forth from the source language, would quite simply fall into the stream unless there were the target language to step onto.

We can only step out of the circle of our language into another circle, another language, Humboldt argues. Such an act should therefore be (as Whorf hoped it would be) an adventure into a conceptual unknown. Though we all live in the same world, stepping into another circle would open up to us (or rather draw us into) another way of seeing, conceiving and experiencing that world. Humboldt, however, is far more tentative than Whorf in estimating how much learning another language can transform our sensitivity and reveal the adopted worldview in its totality:

> To learn a *foreign language* should therefore be to acquire a new standpoint in the world-view hitherto possessed, and in fact to a certain extent it is so, since every language contains the whole conceptual fabric and mode of presentation of a portion of mankind. But because we always carry over, more or less,

our own world-view, and even our own language-view, this outcome is not purely and completely experienced. (ibid.)

Even after speaking a second language for several years, we tend to translate concepts into those of our native tongue, just as we only partially abandon the syntax of our native tongue when we formulate sentences in the foreign language. Though even the first contact with a foreign language can, Humboldt believed, reveal a facet of its incommensurable difference, it is one thing to intuit or form an impression of this difference: it is another to grasp it, to possess it. We can *know* this difference without fully understanding it. In this sense, a language might be compared to someone close to us who, however well we know that individual, remains a mystery to us. We know him without comprehending him. To express this in another analogy, language, like God, *includes* us. To hope to circumscribe the contours of language or of God proves a vain enterprise, though this should hardly discourage us from trying to know either of them better, if knowing implies drawing closer to them.

Considering language as an immobile *object* to be studied proves pointless. This is partly because language is not a static object that can be mastered or a utensil that the language-learner can learn to use. Language remains an individual subjective activity, an interaction. Consequently, any encounter with a foreign language leads us into subjectivity. Repeating a sentence in a foreign language takes us into another mode of perception and conception. This mode can be said to be objective or *trans-subjective* in that it is shared by the individuals of a community, but it is never objective in an impersonal or abstract sense, since our mode of perception and conception is only ever experienced and reaffirmed by individuals who manifest their own personal stance in relation to the worldview of the language in their speech.

Since all objective perception is inevitably tinged with *subjectivity*, we may consider every human individual, even apart from language, as a unique aspect of the world-view. (1999: 59)

What Humboldt calls the character of a language, its individual form of viewing the world, should then be understood as the synthesis of unique individual stances. Character is fluid, and it is, therefore, difficult to grasp. Fragments of the worldview cannot be objectively categorised and catalogued as cartographers would like to organise them. Such cataloguing would only lead to the exhibition of mummies in a museum, and would offer very little insight into language as a living representation of the world. It is because speech and writing always take place in time and space, and imply a stance, a position from which to view or experience the world, that Humboldt suggests that the linguist will profit most by studying individual examples of language in texts, i.e. written discourse.

It is at this stage, however, that the model of languages-as-individuals-with-characters begins to weigh Humboldt down. True, Humboldt is fully aware that this is merely a model to adopt in order to investigate language difference. But he wraps himself up so much in this conceptual model that he begins to attribute to languages as a whole attributes which, by rights, can only be attributed to individual persons. Of Greek and the Greeks, Humboldt affirms, for example:

> Their attention was directed primarily to what things are and how they appear, and not, one-sidedly, to what they count for in the usage of reality. Their bent was therefore originally an *internal* and *intellectual* one. [. . .] In virtue of this mental trait, the Greeks were led by their intellectuality into the whole living multiplicity of the sensuous world, and since they were looking there for something that can only belong to the Idea, were again driven back into intellectuality. (1999: 160–1)

Here Humboldt is affirming something about the psychology of the language and its influence on individual Greeks; but he is also asserting something about the psychology of the Greeks which has gone to produce and sustain this internal and intellectual bent. Such an affirmation might be true of Plato; but was it so of Socrates' wife, who seems to have scorned her husband's philosophising and made it plain she felt he spent too much of his time musing over metaphysics down at the marketplace?

It is not a question of denying the metaphysical élan of Greek philosophers: their contribution to Western thought testifies to the uniqueness of their genius. But in proceeding to define a nation's worldview by referring to individual texts, the individual hides or obscures the society as a whole, the living synthesis of its individuals. The risk is that we will fail to see the wood for the trees, and this risk increases with the greatness of the individual tree. Plato towers above many of the philosophers who came after him. He has come to strike his roots into our own philosophical frameworks and the worldviews of the West so deeply that he tends often to be taken as the epitome of the Greek worldview. But this idea of the philosopher stands at odds with the reality of Greek society in Plato's time. In fact his philosophy was unique and held to be contentious among his peers.

In considering Greek culture we tend to evaluate it as we do any other, i.e. in terms of its use and meaning for us. Greek philosophy was considered to have great meaning for Western cultures in the period preceding and following the birth of Christ, throughout the Medieval period and into the Renaissance and beyond. We have, consequently, tended to reduce Greek culture to what we prize within it, to what we have inherited from it. Here we fall into the trap that Claude Lévi-Strauss identified when he said we evaluate cultures in terms of what they offer us. We fail to understand the meaning of practices, beliefs and institutions for the culture itself, and reduce that culture to what can be collected, exported and consumed. South American cultures were reduced to peanuts and potatoes since these cultures had, unquestionably, made far greater progress in agriculture and selective fertilization than we had (Lévi-Strauss 1961). The meaning that other elements of their culture had for them remains a mystery to us and (if we are honest) leaves most of us indifferent.

Humboldt studies the culture of nations in the great texts that have come down to us, but in comparing different cultures he tends to forget that these texts embody the reflections of outstanding men rather than the ideas of the great majority of individuals who think and feel within a worldview. The same thing can be seen in his comparison of the Romans with the Greeks and the Germans:

Among the Romans, so far as their individuality is also displayed in their language and literature, there is far less evidence of any feeling for the necessity of furnishing the utterances of their mind with any simultaneous direct influence of the impelling and modulating force. Their perfection and greatness develop on another route, more in keeping with the imprint they laid upon their external destinies. By contrast, that feeling speaks out no less plainly, perhaps, in the German temperament than in that of the Greeks, save only that where the latter tended to individualize outer *intuition*, we do so more with inner sensation. (1999: 162)

Did the Roman blacksmith dream of an *external destiny*? Did the Greek cobbler seek to furnish the utterances of his mind with an impelling and modulating force? Does the German accountant seek to express her thought in terms of inner sensation? In a word, we simply do not know. Literature and philosophy may well influence and condition speech and thereby thought (the thinking of individuals and the modes of thinking of the linguistic community as a whole). But in reading the above example we might be forgiven for suspecting that Humboldt has left the blacksmiths, the cobblers and the accountants behind in trying to define the individual characters of nations and their specific worldviews. In Humboldt's reflection quoted above, Greek seems to be incarnated by its philosophy, Latin by its Roman Empire and German by its Storm and Stress and Romantic poetry. Are we talking about the worldview of a language here, or the perspectives of Plato, Caesar and Goethe?

Humboldt's desire to define the characters of languages using the allegorical model of a thinking, feeling individual induces him to make some sweeping statements about the nature of languages and peoples which will appear at times grotesque and absurd. Humboldt reasons, for example, that:

Should not, for example, the fine distinctions of numerous modifications and positionings of the vowel, and the meaningful use of these, coupled with a restriction to this procedure and a rejection of compounding, betray and promote an excess of clever and crafty analytical understanding among the peoples of Semitic descent, especially the Arabs? (162)

Humboldt may well be right to stress the importance of the intuitive impression we have of a foreign language, as we try to take on board the differences of organisation and conceptualisation which it imposes upon us and as we try to learn to make sense of what we hear and read. But by plunging into texts of a very specific nature and trying to gain from them a view of the language as a whole, there is an obvious danger of confusing the exceptional with that which is common to all and representative of the whole. Reading Goethe may indeed teach the English-speaker to see the world anew, just as Germans sometimes claim Shakespeare has taught them to see the world anew, but reading Goethe does not necessarily reveal to us how most Germans see the world they live in.

It would seem, therefore, that Humboldt's admiration for the texts he studied, and the enthusiasm with which he tried to grasp their meaning, sometimes misled him into taking his fragments for the whole. Ultimately, the strangeness that we experience as we move into the worldview as it is expressed in a text, is partly the result of the strangeness of the language, partly the result of the strangeness of the period in which the text was written, and partly the result of the uniqueness of the individual worldview of the writer as he unfolds his perception of people, events, circumstances and ideas. Humboldt was extremely sensitive to the way in which a language was created and sustained by the individual's speech and the way it was shaped and reshaped over time by individuals. But, as the above examples show, at times, he would reduce the character of the language to the character of the individual.

CHAPTER 13

A Seeing and Feeling Worldview

As we saw in the last chapter, we are faced then with two equally unsatisfactory extremes when it comes to comparing languages. On the one hand, the fragment can obscure the whole: taking Plato's Greek to be a representative fragment of the Greek worldview can mislead us. On the other hand, the failure to focus on the parts of the whole (i.e. individual discourse) can lead us into a formal understanding which is not merely superficial but indeed blind to the actual nature of language as the means by which individuals express meaning.

The comparison of worldviews, if that is to become our project, is also hampered by the very term *worldview*. The term, as we have seen, has two clearly separate meanings. As *Weltansicht*, it is the patterning of conceptual frameworks and the organisation of ideas which makes up the form of the language (in Humboldt's definition of form), the patterning within which we think and without which we cannot think in any conceptual or sophisticated manner. In *Weltanschauung*, it is the intellectual refinement and elaboration of those fundamental conceptual frameworks which enable us to give form to various mindsets or ideologies. The first notion of worldview (*Weltansicht*) implies the socially constructed formation of the individual's mind and his linguistic capacity. The second (*Weltanschauung*) implies the construction of various kinds of world-conceptions which takes place in our speech with others.

In Chapter 7, in our discussion of definitions for 'worldview', we considered Klemperer's example of the shopkeeper with his Nazi *Weltanschauung*. We might say that the worldview that the shopkeeper proudly laid claim to was partly personal and partly party-doctrine, but both went to form his own manner of perceiving and conceiving the political and social world around him. This personal worldview must be contrasted to the more fundamental worldview which Humboldt would have called *Weltansicht*, the organisation of concepts, connections and frameworks within the German language. This framework of patterning, manifest in the German language system as a whole, was what allowed Communists and Christians alike to perceive and conceive the world around themselves in a very different manner to the Nazi party member.

This distinction is fundamental. But even the very etymological and morphological composition of the terms *Weltansicht* and *Weltanschauung* is problematic. The form of the words reveals only too well the conceptual model which generated them. *Weltansicht* and *Weltanschauung*, like the English term 'worldview', derive from the representation of perception in terms of seeing. Seeing is, of course, one of the fundamental senses by which we come to know the world, so in one sense to say 'seeing is knowing' is not a metaphor. But it becomes a metaphor as soon as we say *I see what you mean*, or *I see the difference between the two ideas*. In both instances, knowing has been subsumed within the metaphor, knowing = seeing.

This metaphor does not begin with Humboldt or Kant of course. Indeed Eve Sweetser (1990: 32–4) has traced it back through Indo-European languages. The results of this fascinating piece of linguistic archaeology are worth quoting. Starting off with the reconstructed root of the verb *to see* in Indo-European, **weid-*, Sweetser traces the way this root has developed into Greek to provide both *eidon* (to see) and *oida* (to know), from which we derive our English word, *idea*. In English, the **weid-* root forms the basis of words such as *to witness* (to know by having seen something), but also *wit* and *wise*. Amusingly for us today, **weid-* also resurfaced in the Latin word for the verb to see, *video*, which English-speakers have exploited and introduced to so many other languages in its contemporary meaning (video cassettes).

As Sweetser demonstrates, seeing and knowing are not only metaphorically linked: their connection has helped shape and structure the words (and therefore the concepts) we use to speak about our way of seeing and knowing the world. Etymology can, in this sense, reveal the fabric of frameworks which formed our concepts. The relationship between seeing and knowing seems then to be a very rich and ancient one which echoes within the various languages to which English is related.

Nevertheless, the fact that our term *worldview* highlights seeing over other senses is particularly unfortunate in Humboldt's work because it tends to obscure part of the richness of his conceptualisation of speech. Humboldt always stresses not only the intellectual aspect of language but also its physical reality. Language is sensuous in the very act of speech, because we use our physical faculties to hear and speak. The very structuring of our concepts also reflects and engenders frameworks of a sensuous nature. Language cultivates distinctions in, and categories of, taste and touch and hearing. Language offers an infinite variety of ways in which we can categorise and combine concepts in order to define experiences of non-visual perception.

We can invent complex or paradoxical categories: we can say that a salad dressing is bitter-sweet, for example. We can extend immediate perception of physical reality to speak of the nature or character of a person: we can say a person is *touchy*, for example. But this is not all. We speak of our senses in metaphoric ways in order to attain a heightened precision of expression. We speak of words which sound *bitter*. We speak of *loud colours*. A slightly more original example would be, *Her honey-like voice caressed me*. Here, sound is translated into taste which can touch us. This expression of one experience using another one of our senses is called synaesthesia.

It might be argued that this is a poetic use of language, but if this is so, then it is poetry of a kind that animates and structures everyday language, because such expressions are commonplace throughout languages. We can, for example, find analogues to the English expression *facing the bitter truth*. In French we speak of *l'âpre vérité* and in Czech we speak of the *trpká pravda* (both of which expressions translate into English as 'bitter truth'). In German, we use an expression which can be translated as 'to swallow a bitter pill' (*die bittere Pille schlucken*).

Humboldt was very much alive to this sensuous reality which is found within language and which radiates within the thinking, feeling consciousness of the people who speak it. This is the reality which language as a living expression of human thought reflects, but also the reality which language draws us towards. Language not only reveals something about the way individuals and linguistic communities think. Language also educates us (or sensitises us) to the world around us, since often having a means of expression for a thing or an experience, heightens our experience of that thing or experience. Poets or singers, for example, help us understand what is happening to us when we fall in love. But on a much more prosaic level, the butcher's son or daughter learns to see and to know intimately the carcass of the bull or the sheep, where most people notice only a mass of meat and bones. This is not only because the butcher's son learns to observe meat and its dissection, but because the vocabulary he hears directs his inquiring eyes as he begins to set up for himself the categories he uses to order and interpret the things that exist within his personal space. The child of a lumber-jack will see a wide variety of oaks, elms and birches in different stages of growth and hear the songs of chaffinches, wood-pigeons and blackbirds, where the average city-dweller, walking through the same woods will see only a mass of colourful trees and hear a symphony of birds.

There is nothing particularly romantic or idealistic in this idea. Children and adolescents who move from town to country (or vice versa) find it astounding and laughable that those of the same age as them are wholly ignorant of many facets of their own experience of reality. When they express the fact that their peers *cannot get their heads around something*, they are referring not only to a lack of knowledge but also a lack of vocabulary and the lack of any means of structuring their own categories of experience. Ultimately, it would seem that a lack of knowledge and a lack of vocabulary prevent perception and sensitivity from being cultivated to their full potential while terms and the understanding that goes with them predispose the individual to a more heightened perception of reality. Words and expressions thus not only allow us to show something, they often allow us to learn and know something. In this sense, the cultivation of man takes place within language (though it would be absurd to separate language from reality and to claim that we cannot really feel something without the intervention of language). We think within language, and live within the world (in which language crystallises, channels and frames our thought and perception).

This cultivation, by which is meant the refinement of the faculty by which we know the world, cannot be reduced to a mere intellectual or conceptual form of knowing: neither can it be reduced to the single sense of sight. For this reason it might be wiser to replace *worldview* (*Weltansicht*), with a more appropriate term. Indeed, I would propose two terms, *world-perceiving* and *world-conceiving*. The former could be used to designate the process by which we actively perceive the world; the second would designate the process by which we intellectualise and organise what we perceive.

I have purposely avoided using nouns (i.e. world-perception, and world-conception) to stress the ongoing and dynamic process by which worldviews are formed and sustained. Sometimes, the term worldview is considered to represent a fixed point of view, and there has been much mistrust of the term on this account. It is often assumed that there is something deterministic in the term worldview, i.e. that in channelling perception, it harnesses, directs and thereby limits perception. Harnessing implies that we become in some way slaves to a personified all-controlling language. In such a model, language directs us just as the rider harnesses his horse. Such a view of worldview is far removed from Humboldt's conception of language, however. For Humboldt we always perceive things from a given position. Perception changes as we move, and language moves as we move.

This fluidity of language can hardly facilitate the task of catching the character of any given language, however. How can we pin it down if it is always moving? How can we define its overall or essential nature if it is deeply personal and subjective? If words are not concrete things but rather, 'the resting place' for the soul's inner activity (Humboldt 1999: 92), how can we hope to catch a glimpse of the way people perceive and conceive of the world by combining words together in their speech?

The task would seem all but impossible and vain, if it were not for the fact that each time we try to learn a foreign language we are confronted by an incommensurable difference in the way the new language organises its terms and in the way it combines its concepts in order to structure its representation of the real world of its speakers. This strangeness testifies to the difference of that language, and it would seem to promise we might in fact be able to catch a glimpse of one facet of its worldview.

The truth of this experience can be verified if we take up the different way concepts are formed and used to form related concepts in various languages: Let's take the concept of *truth* itself for our example. If we restrict our consideration of truth to four Indo-European languages, English, French, German and Czech, we will find the respective words, *vérité*, *Wahrheit* and *pravda*, coincide to a large extent. Truth can be *found*, *verified* and *established* in all four languages.

However, with study, we soon find that our word for truth will not always translate directly into the expressions found in the other three languages. While we can say we *penetrate the truth* in English and while the French can translate this expression (*pénétrer la vérité*), this expression is uncommon in German and is unknown in Czech. In Czech, in contrast, one can *have truth* (*mít pravdu*) while in English we conceive of this state in terms of *being right*. In English we say one *is right* or one is *in the right*. In German, one says *Du hast recht* (You have right). French reveals a predilection for reason over right in conceiving the roughly equivalent idea in the following terms: *Tu as raison*.

In a similar manner, truth explores different conceptual trajectories in the lexicons of the four languages. It will no doubt strike the English-speaker as strange that the equivalent word for *truth* forms the root of our word for *likely* in French (*vraisemblable*), and the root for our word for *fortune-teller* in German (*Wahrsager/Wahrsagerin*). Striking differences in the metaphorical expressions to be found in the four languages also appear when the word *truth* is compared. We can say we *serve truth* in English, French and German. So why is this expression not to be found in Czech? What does this tell us about the nature of Czech culture and the character of the Czech worldview?

This brief example only scratches the surface of the concepts of truth as they are constructed in the four languages, but it should suffice to demonstrate the difficulty with which all language-learners are faced when they choose to open up to another language. Attempting to master another language involves not only mastering the grammatical rules and learning the vocabulary, but also remodelling the conceptual frameworks with which and within which we think. It takes considerable effort to leave behind the naïve idea that concepts can be translated directly from one language to another, but the further we navigate into the foreign waters of another language, the more we realise that coming to terms with that tongue involves charting courses taken by creative, thinking men as their minds struggled to open up modes of expression. Often those modes of expression have followed similar courses in our own language, but at times the paths they took lead us elsewhere. At such moments we are left facing the shapes and forms of the foreign conceptual logic feeling lost and confused. We find it almost impossible to break out of the course of conceptual reasoning that our native tongue frames for us. This is the no man's land that the language-learner must learn to live in. This common experience is the act of confronting a foreign worldview (*Weltansicht*). Learning to provisionally abandon the signposts of our own language in order to follow the logic of another creative formulation of a concept means taking one step towards grasping the character of a language.

CHAPTER 14

Four Dangers in the Comparative Approach

In the last chapter we considered the experience of confronting a foreign worldview and attempting to come to terms with a language's character. The difficulty of the task should not be underestimated. Humboldt himself always stressed that his form of comparative philology would be both laborious and inconclusive. No doubt it would be wise to consider the failure met by others who have striven to make a meaningful contribution to the comparison of languages, before setting off unwittingly to make the same mistakes ourselves. Four forms of error lie in wait for anyone who embarks upon the comparison of languages. These errors concern terms, scope, methodology and motivation.

Firstly, the terms of the debate may be ill-defined. This question has already been partially clarified in the discussion of thought, language and worldview, but it will require further consideration in Chapter 15 which (it is hoped) will serve to refine our terms for speaking about language, and worldview.

Secondly, the scope of the study may blind us to truths about the natures of the languages studied or lead us to misconstrue the aspects we study. This can be seen when Humboldt himself confuses the writings of great writers with the language as a whole within which the writer expressed himself; e.g. confusing Shakespeare's English with English or Goethe's German with German. It can also be seen when we multiply the languages compared, treating them more and more superficially, the more languages we take on board.

Thirdly, the methodology by which we compare languages may be at fault. Are we comparing one language in terms of another, rather than examining it in terms of its own inner logic? This error can be found in French studies of German, for example, which refer to the *inversion* to be found in German syntax which puts the verb at the end of the subordinate clause. The term *inversion* implies that German in some way *should be* structured in the same way as French and that it *deviates* from a logical pattern. In such comparisons, the logic of one language is obscured when it is conceived in terms of the logic of another.

Fourthly, the desire to compare languages should be questioned and analysed. Why do we wish to compare languages? What are we trying to prove? Should we be trying to prove anything? Are we really proceeding in an empirical manner, objectively assembling data and allowing that data to form itself into similarities and dissimilarities which reflect the true aspects of the languages studied? Our reasons for comparing languages may be perfectly legitimate philological reasons. On the other hand, an unacknowledged (and often unwitting) bias and chauvinism at times hide behind what first appear to be erudite and scientific investigations into linguistic difference.

Meschonnic, in his book-length study *De la langue française* (1997), quotes examples of comparisons which show that multiple errors can be combined to produce the most curious of conclusions. Often the desire to celebrate one language (and thereby champion it in relation to others) combines with a fanciful metaphorical flourish. Languages are compared to rivers and to women, among other things. This use of figurative language *disfigures* the debate, but this is not only because it leads us to confuse the object of study, the language, with the metaphorical model, but also because this playful allegory begins to impose itself upon us and to structure the way we understand the language and, more importantly, which parts of it we see. Meschonnic satirises Dominique Bouhours, a French Jesuit grammarian of the seventeenth century, for example, for whom Spanish is like the enormous agitated rivers of that country while Italian is like those agreeable streams that gargle among the pebbles of a prairie valley but which at times grow great enough to flood the whole countryside (Meschonnic 1997: 256, mT). French, for this

Frenchman, was in contrast like those great rivers that enrich all the places through which they pass.

It would be pedantic to point out that Bouhours' botany and geography were no stronger than his linguistics. (All rivers and streams enrich the land they pass through.) Nonetheless, the example of Bouhours quoted by Meschonnic allows us to signpost several mistakes which should be avoided when comparing languages. We should strive to say what we mean and avoid unnecessary metaphorical or allegorical thinking. And we should refuse to allow the frameworks of our models or representations to impose their categories upon the object of study. If there is no river to represent Czech or Finnish in Bouhours' botany, for example, this will seriously limit his reverie. Categories and frameworks of understanding which enslave us to inapt metaphors distort our perception and conception.

Patriotism (or chauvinism rather) is an obvious danger when comparing languages. Misleadingly flattering celebrations will always be met with applause by the public who feel (as the members of all linguistic communities feel) that their language is one of infinite richness, diversity and complexity. Inverted patriotism is not rare, however, and translators, men and women who strike out across the linguistic frontiers, are often inclined to justify their work (which they themselves appear to feel is unsatisfactory) by claiming that their own language lacks the subtlety and richness of their chosen second language. It is not, they seem to argue, their fault if their translations pale in comparison to the genius of the originals. The raw materials which they are forced to make use of are inadequate.

In such cases translators invariably confuse the adopted language (the shared work of a linguistic community) with the specific use of that language by the creative mind which they are attempting to convey in another tongue. They assume their author incarnates the essence of his language. This, in itself, is spurious. Baudelaire may be poetic, French is not necessarily so. Conveying Baudelaire's poetry into English, is, of course, no easy matter. Translation always remains a creative, if a rigorous, activity; the creation should to some extent transform the target language and enhance its vigour as a means of expression. Shakespeare requires a translator with the same genius as himself – a daunting challenge. But Shakespeare's genius in no way proves the poverty of the language of Luther, simply because no German translation is considered to measure up to the original. Celebrations of languages born of inverted chauvinism are of no more use to us in comparing languages than the chauvinistic declarations of those who claim their own language surpasses in richness all others. Those who celebrate their own language invariably compare it to languages they do not know, while those who have fallen in love with a foreign language often suffer from a feeling of ambivalence to their own language which, in the glare of their love of the foreign, is shrugged off into the shadows.

For Meschonnic 'all comparison reveals or hides an evalutation' (1997: 257, mT). In his *Critique du rythme* (1982), Meschonnic quotes the example of A. W. Schlegel, the German philologist, a contemporary of Humboldt who introduced a curious aesthetic theory of languages. His theorisation of euphony and cacophony in languages was based upon a distinction which he made between the functions of the vowel and the consonant in languages. For Schlegel, consonants contributed more to representation (*das Darstellende*), while vowels contributed more to expression (*das Ausdrückende*) in language. According to Schlegel, the euphony of a language depended upon the degree to which it was softened by its vowels, the ideal being a balance between consonants and vowels. Since Germanic languages were heavily weighted by consonants, even High German was considered by Schlegel to be unfortunate in its form, while the Slavic language which he attributed to Bohemia (but by which he probably meant Polish) was much worse since it permitted entire words without vowels, as can be seen in his example of *Przmysl* (Meschonnic 1982: 421).

Schlegel provides us with an example of a learned or erudite defence of what comes down to a question of taste. Can we justify linguistically preferring one language over another? Are there criteria by which we can assess the inner harmony of languages and according to which we can evaluate their worth? Can we order languages in aesthetic hierarchies? Certainly, Schlegel seemed to think so. And in his defence of his stance he armed himself with analytical ammunition. But the objective analysis of morphology should not blind us to the arbitrary subjective nature of the grounds upon which Schlegel's aesthetic judgement is based.

We can find parallels to Schlegel's learned defence in much more prosaic quarters. A similar account can be found in contemporary France, in which French is held by many French-speakers to be rich and poetic, while English, it is argued, is more apt for discussing concrete, everyday things (business, in short). The fact that English is the business language of the world comforts such people in this binary opposition, though the fact that Shakespeare was not French will no doubt be discreetly pushed to one side by those who wish to champion French as the language of poetry.

Even when we do not seek to champion one language over another though, even when we sincerely strive to maintain an objective empirical treatment of languages, the scope of the comparison can deform our perception of what is considered. An instructive example can be found in contemporary translation studies. The work on comparative stylistics done by Vinay and Darbelnet (1958), which aims to render the translator and the student of translation sensitive to differences in usage in English and French, has understandably been of great influence in recent decades, and Guillemin-Flescher (1981) has shown ways in which the project can be extended to concentrate on syntax in order to show the way the two languages foreground meaning using different means. However, all three linguists do at times fall into the trap of opposing English and French rather than simply comparing them. The effect of contrasting does in fact tend to induce us into taking differences for oppositions. As a result, Vinay and Darbelnet will, for example, consider French to be abstract while English, they claim, is concrete. They base such a claim on the fact that in French there is a tendency to privilege nouns, while in English it is more common to have recourse to a verb. Vinay and Darbelnet provide much convincing evidence to support such a claim. We will speak of the *coming down the mountain* while a Frenchman will speak of *la descente de la montagne* (the descent from the mountain). In English, Vinay and Darbelnet will point to the prepositions used to form phrasal verbs as grammatical units which fix the action spatially, while in French, other less direct forms are used. We say for example *to turn round*, while the French say *se retourner*. This physical aspect remains explicit in more abstract verbs: we say for example *to cut down on one's spending*, while the French will express the same idea without having recourse to a preposition (*réduire ses dépenses*).

The importance of highlighting such distinctions is, of course, capital for anyone teaching translation, but the conclusion that one language is abstract while another is concrete requires far stronger evidence. Invariably, the use of a noun in English is one of various possible options, and these options correspond to different registers. To use the noun in the sentence *The descent from the mountain* would indeed seem to render the English sentence more abstract, but it is perfectly correct idiomatically speaking. In the same way, the French can opt for a more visual representation in the sentence, *pendant qu'il descendait de la montagne.* This would situate the idea in a more concrete context.

Nouns are indeed an indication of a level of abstraction in that they distance us from the subject-verb-object phrase in which we can imagine someone doing something. But *nominalisation* is in fact common in English in jargon and technical language. Ironically, many of the nouns found in English technical jargon are imposing new noun forms in French as this language struggles to absorb new concepts and terms borrowed from English.

To claim that English is less abstract than French appears to be unfounded for two reasons: firstly, it seems to imply that philosophy would be impossible in English, and secondly, it seems to imply that French is somehow inept in expressing everyday experience. Is the Vinay-Darbelnet hypothesis not rather one of those rigorously erudite attempts to bolster a commonly believed prejudice, the 'scientific elaboration' of an unfounded cliché? If this is so, then they are victims of the fourth error we mentioned above: failing to perceive your own reasons for wishing to compare languages.

Even though Vinay and Darbelnet might seem to be handing out the roses equally to each of the contenders, there is an implicit evaluation in claiming one language is more apt for expressing ideas and another for expressing the world of things. The grotesque opposition which emerges from this biased analysis is perhaps a consequence of the limited scope of the comparison. Comparing two things tends to highlight their dissimilarities while pushing into the shadows their similarities. If we hold an orange up next to an apple we notice that one is orange while the other is green (or red). We are less likely to consider that both are sweet, contain vitamin C and have pips. Binary comparisons highlight contrasts. In order to avoid the distortion caused by exaggerating the importance of contrasts, all we need to do is to introduce a third term to explode the simplistic oppositions that seem to impose themselves as self-evident truths. A tripartite model makes simplistic oppositions (such as the one Vinay and Darbelnet posit) impossible. In the abstract-concrete hypothesis, where can we situate Spanish or German, for example? Would the authors ever have felt inclined towards opposition if they had chosen to study three or more languages?

Humboldt's study of language was of far greater scope. He learnt languages throughout his life, and his career as a diplomat led him to live abroad and forced him to mix in multicultural gatherings. He was certainly not inclined towards simplistic binary oppositions. Nor was he tempted by vulgar celebrations of one language over another, though this was a common *jeu de société* in the circles within which he moved. He was certainly no relativist, and in fact his evaluation of languages coincides to a large extent with the time and culture to which he belonged. Educated Germans of that period admired French but were looking for an alternative source of inspiration to French or to Latin (which had been, so to speak, adopted by French as its *Latin mother*). German could not claim to be the daughter of Latin. Germans were, consequently, drawn towards Greek, and claims that there is an intimate relationship or similarity between the two languages – an unsubstantiated claim – were not uncommon throughout the nineteenth and twentieth centuries in Germany. Sanskrit was being studied by Humboldt's peers. All of these influences contributed to Humboldt's sensitivity to languages and cultivated his taste. His taste inevitably affected his judgements about languages. Yet throughout his work, Humboldt seems to relish each language he discovers and always seems to seek to discern the subtle richness of the modes by which it has resolved the questions of denomination and conceptualisation, and the ways the parts of the language are configured to form the whole. If at times he allows his enthusiasm for individual discourse to obscure the image he presents of a language as a whole, then it is because he is fascinated by the way genius (i.e. the intense work of the spirit) transforms and maintains language and makes it what it is, an astoundingly refined and *refinable* working apparatus for perceiving, conceiving the world and speaking about it.

CHAPTER 15

Reformulating the Worldview Hypothesis

If Humboldt's dual concern for the human faculty of language and for the comparison of different language systems is a difficult and daunting one, then the enormity of the task of grasping a language's character and comparing it with another should instil in us a sense of humility. We cannot hope to fit into boxes the language which contains us, our thoughts and all we say. Comparing languages will not provide us with an assortment of boxes which we can order in some conceptual warehouse. And yet, the desire to find some kind of order among the infinite variety of languages, the attempt to seize something of the organising principle of different languages, animated Humboldt. In his attempt to achieve a fragmentary insight into the hidden whole of a language (a whole which was to some extent manifest in the interaction of the parts of individual texts), he hoped to form an idea not only of the way each language worked but also the way language as a human faculty evolves.

The present contribution to the Humboldtian project is a modest one: it aims to take up the concepts which we have used in English to speak about the relationship between language, thought and worldview, in order to reveal the instability and vagueness of these terms before returning to alternative formulations of that relationship. Given the unquestionable difficulty of comparing languages, it surely seems unwise to embark upon a Humboldt-inspired project without first clarifying our terms.

Before looking more closely at the definitions I shall be introducing, let's summarise the contribution of Humboldt's approach to language. Humboldt takes us forward in our project to consider the relationship between language and worldview for six reasons:

1. His concept of *Weltansicht* coupled with Trabant's *Weltanschauung–Weltansicht* distinction enable us to radically reappraise our concept of worldview by distinguishing between:

    a. the organised conceptual frameworks which are necessary for an individual to take the world into him- or herself and understand it, and

    b. the shared conception of the world and the shared ideas and customary beliefs of a group which are generated in and by individuals' discussion. It is this shared conception which allows us to maintain that one group of people understands the world in a radically different manner than another group although they both belong to the same linguistic community.

2. Humboldt integrates the Kantian refinement of perception as an active process, a process which involves judgement and conception. Humboldt went on to situate the cultivation of perception within the framework of language, though he never conceived of language as a barrier between individuals and the world they perceived.

3. Humboldt stressed that language, far from being a deterministic force, a controlling influence, which imposed itself upon men and women, was the work of individual minds, the sum total of the imprints people left behind them after they had struggled to express themselves in speech.

4. Since Humboldt stressed the importance of individual creativity for fashioning language and maintaining its élan as a living mode of expression, he held in high esteem poets, writers and philosophers. These, he argued, contributed to innovation and to the renovation and regeneration of language.

5. Humboldt transcended the form–sense opposition which tends to induce many linguists to reduce languages in comparative study to their grammatical form. Humboldt maintained that

speech was always meaningful and if linguistic study was not to become meaningless, it should never lose sight of this fact. For this reason he considered the study of grammatical form, as some supra- or trans-semantic element (an inner core), to be only one aspect of linguistics among others. The study of the inner core or formal grammar of a language could only ever hope to outline the skeleton of a language. In contrast to this, Humboldt stressed the importance of studying the way texts and speech generate meaning. In this sense, his notion of form can be considered to be the organisation of meaning, as we, the speakers of a nation (or linguistic community), inherit it. Form, for Humboldt, far from existing above individuals or below or behind speech, was to be found in usage and only in usage. And the rules we assimilate are transmitted to us through our comprehension of the speech and writing of individuals.

6. Humboldt contended that just as people became cultivated with and within language, they simultaneously cultivated language by leaving their own personal impressions upon it. Consequently, different languages evolved along different lines, developing a greater or lesser sensitivity to the world in which they were rooted thanks to the cumulative influence of the work of individual minds in their struggle to find expression in speech.

For all these reasons, Humboldt's contribution to the concept of worldview should be an enriching and thought-provoking one. Humboldt's approach should keep us from trying to understand the subjective experience of making meaning with the tools of an objectivist scientific approach. This should allow us to escape the mania for categorisation and enable us to reconsider the way we conceptualise the world we live in. By rigorously analysing the different formulations of meaning to be found in various languages and by studying the different trajectories those languages take in striking their roots into reality, we might hope to conceive of a more accurate, more genuine and more meaningful model of a language's character and the worldview it constitutes. But before returning to the comparative study of languages, we must first turn to the terms of our debate.

In the course of this short study four terms, *world*, *worldview*, *thought* and *language* have emerged as particularly problematic concepts which may be said to harbour multiple meanings. Their polysemy makes their use in discourse often ambiguous. These terms are shown together below as overlapping spheres of meaning in order to stress the way each of the four terms enters into the semantic sphere of the other three terms:

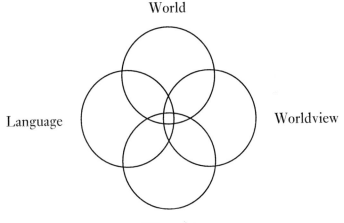

As a German thinker of the early nineteenth century, Humboldt can hardly be expected to resolve the problems of English definitions, but until we ourselves address these problems our attempts to make a meaningful contribution to the worldview question will remain vague and unconvincing. For this reason, the following sections will be devoted to redefining the four key terms of our debate.

WORLD

World has multiple meanings, as do its equivalent terms in other languages (*monde*, in French, *Welt*, in German, *svět*, in Czech, for example). We use *world* in English to mean:

- the earth
- the universe
- the system of things

- the present state of existence (*this world* as opposed to *the next one*, or *the metaphysical world*)
- public life or society
- a sphere of interest or activity (*the world of finance*, for example)
- an extensive land mass (*The New World*, for example).

Analogous usages will be found in many other languages, and this polysemy causes no difficulty of understanding because the context usually makes it clear which meaning is intended. Invariably, if terms become confused in common speech, a distinction is invented. But these different meanings of *world* seem to coexist quite happily in everyday language, by attaching themselves to one single multi-purpose signifier. Similarly, metaphoric uses of the term, like the following one, are understood with no difficulty: *The couple became estranged and soon the two were **worlds apart**.*

The term *world* becomes problematic, however, in precisely the sphere in which we try to determine the relationship between language and the world. Trabant is struggling with the difficult task of expressing this relationship when he suggests that 'languages give us the world, in a certain manner . . . in order to allow us to speak about it' (1992: 56, mT). *Giving*, for Trabant, has to be understood as the act of perceiving the world and elaborating the concepts necessary to speak about it. It would be absurd to misread Trabant's sentence, by claiming that language allows us to possess the world, in some way, as, for instance, we can possess an apple. Trabant's is a meaningful attempt to clarify something obscure.

Fuzzy or sloppy definitions are not rare, however, when languages are compared. The title of Stamm's book *The Word is a World* (*La parole est un monde*) is an act of poetic obfuscation, for example. In her attempt to dramatise the importance of language, Stamm absurdly accords equal value to one aspect of it (the word) and to the whole of life as we know it (the world). Such confusions are not restricted to naïve enthusiasts of language. Though George Steiner should not be confused with Anne Stamm, his claim that 'language makes man at home in the world . . .' (Steiner 1975: 86) certainly requires some clarification. Here, Steiner seems to be claiming that we recognise the world around us through language, because our language is the means by which we familiarise ourselves with the things that surround us. Children, for example, learn to distinguish between the oak and the silver birch by collecting their leaves and learning their names. They learn to distinguish between books and magazines when their parents correct their use of their expanding but insufficient conceptual categories. It is indeed difficult to imagine how anyone deprived of language could live comfortably in the world. Nevertheless, language is not the sole thing that allows us to find or form a place in the world. Family, friends and work and colleagues are only some of the elements that contribute to forming and maintaining our identity in the world. And though family, friends, work and colleagues are inseparable from speech, they cannot be reduced to language. To see them exclusively through the prism of linguistics would be both perverse and absurd. A clearer or more apt reformulation of Steiner's position would be: language enables man to find his place in the world by defining himself and his relationship to things and to other people by virtue of his faculty of speech.

In order to avoid any unnecessary squabbling between academics of different disciplines, it would seem wise to avoid obscure and hyperbolic language when speaking of the individual's relationship to the world and the role language plays in the development of that relationship. To claim that an individual cannot know the world without language (a common enough claim among contemporary linguists) is needlessly provocative. Language may well influence perception, but perception cannot be reduced to a sub-category of linguistics. In seeking to extol their chosen discipline, linguists who take this line refuse to define exactly what they mean by *knowing the world*. Few would deny that we can distinguish between tastes, colours or textures without the vocabulary necessary to express our experience of them, though vocabulary may well direct and refine our perception of those tastes, colours and textures.

Until a distinction is made between knowing the world physically and knowing it conceptually, philosophers might conclude that linguists are existentialists when they suggest we need language in order to know the world. This would be a curious misinterpretation of Humboldt's own stance. Existentialism is generally opposed to rationalist and empiricist philosophies which assume that the universe is a determined, ordered system intelligible to the contemplative observer who can discover the natural laws that govern all beings and the role of reason as the power guiding human activity (Flew 1979: 115). Though it is true that both Kant and Humboldt in their own ways circumscribed the limits of Reason's power to interpret and categorise the world and our experience of it, neither considered the investigation of the world through language to be a wild-goose chase.

Language is a system by which men and women make sense of the world and express their interpretations of it. If speakers did not believe it were possible to describe the world and their own place in it in an accurate and meaningful way, their words would be meaningless and their attempts to communicate their intentions would be vain. Comparing languages introduces us into different manners of describing the world. Though these modes of description may vary, it does not follow that the world itself cannot be known, but simply that different aspects of the world and our relationship to it are highlighted in different language systems.

In order to avoid ill-founded accusations of existentialism, we need to make a clear distinction between *the world as it is* and *our representation of the world*. Most people consider there to be a world around us, in which we live, the world we perceive with our senses. This is the 'real' world of which we speak when we open our mouths. This is the world that, since Aristotle at least, men have investigated and tried to define. And most people hold that the definitions and categories in our language do indeed correspond to the reality outside of our senses, and are not simply arbitrary arrangements imposed upon our perception by language. Dolphins are not fish. Bats are not birds. Scientific investigation can only be meaningful if we believe that we can perceive and describe the things around us and the relationships between them.

In contrast to this real existing world, there is, however, the world as we perceive it. Perception, as has been said, is a partially active process and language does contribute to the way in which our perception of the real existing world is directed and shaped. In this way, perception is influenced by the representation of the world which our language opens up to us. For example, our knowledge of the world is inscribed in the organising concepts we think with. To someone unfamiliar with birds, the crow and the raven may seem indistinguishable, but the fact that we consider them as distinct species alerts us to the fact that some fundamental difference between the two must exist. Observation of the two will reveal to us, for example, that crows are solitary, ravens are gregarious. Perception clearly precedes and transcends language, however. We do not need to know the word *toothache* to feel what we designate by that term (though we do, of course, need to be able to describe the sensation when we seek relief from that pain when we go to see a dentist).

In addition to the world of objective reality, the world we perceive, and the world we learn to conceive though our faculty of speech, there is a third concept of world: this is the *world* that comes into play in discussions of the relationship between language and reality: *the world of which we speak.* The way we define our lives, our existences, our aspirations and our hopes and dreams are shaped together as we discuss the world with others. Whether we are Platonists who believe man lives in a cave-like prison, cut off from the transcendental reality of the true forms, or materialists who believe that man should seek satisfaction in the here and now since that is all that exists, all of our discussions of the real existing world take place within language, and it is through learning language and through reshaping it to fit our own experience of the world, that we come to define it for ourselves. *The world of which we speak* implies not only dialogue with others but also that internal monologue that takes place as we assimilate, contemplate and react to what we hear in conversation with others.

The world of which we speak involves belief systems, and the shared constructed systems of thinking which are common to communities, classes and groups of different types and of different ages. Such systems order the fundamental concepts of the worldview of different groups along different lines. Class, for example, in monarchic and capitalist societies tends to be conceived along the lines of a hierarchical spatial metaphor system which is implicitly value-oriented. For this reason, translating a phrase (which might to some seem innocent enough) such as *the lower classes* becomes problematic when the target culture is Soviet Russia. The French Prime Minister in 2002, Raffarin, saw nothing amiss in claiming that it was the duty of his right-wing Republican party *to aid the French at the bottom* (*aider les français d'en bas*). Just as Raffarin unwittingly insulted those he intended to reassure, the translator who represents the working classes as the lower classes in a culture which extols the worker as the model citizen, is unlikely to meet with a warm welcome. Indeed the equivalents of both *lower* and *upper* classes were actively edited out of Communist publications in Czech after the party took power in Czechoslovakia in 1948 (though in post-1989 Czech society equivalents for *upper class* are making a come back). What this shows is that class is not only a social and cultural phenomenon, but also a linguistic construct. The way we speak about the world, it would seem, is influenced by conceptions we adopt unwittingly as we accept words and phrases in common usage.

If we are to speak clearly about the way language influences our view of the world, we should make it clear whether we are speaking of:

1. the objective world,
2. the world as we perceive it, or
3. the world as we as individuals and groups conceive it when we speak about it.

LANGUAGE

The term *language* also requires some clarification. In contrast to the term *world*, *language* does not translate easily into other languages. The multiple meanings of the English term do not coincide with the multiple meanings of words such as *langue* and *langage*, in French, *Sprache* and *Rede*, in German, or *jazyk* and *řeč*, in Czech. Nevertheless, the English language does provide sufficient means to distinguish between the several usages of our term, and it will suffice to make use of them to avoid misconceptions. *Language* in English is used to mean:

• the faculty of human speech
• a variety of speech or body of words belonging to a linguistic community or nation (English or French, for example)
• diction or style of speech, the use of language common to a person, group or class.

It is this last definition that we have in mind when we speak of Blair's English or Shakespeare's English. Using other terms such as *dialogue*, *conversation* and *speech act* should also help avoid confusing different meanings of the word *speech*. Such definitions are obvious enough, and discussing them would be pointless were it not for the fact that uses of the words *speech* and *language* often allow great scope for interpretation. A few examples should make this clear.

The British psychiatrist, Theodore Dalrymple, in his *Life at the Bottom: The Worldview that Makes the Underclass* (2001) has something specific in mind when he claims worldviews and language are related:

> [. . .] everyone has a Weltanschauung, a worldview, whether he knows it or not. [. . .] Their ideas make themselves manifest even in the language they use. The frequency of locutions of passivity is a striking example. An alcoholic, explaining his misconduct while drunk, will say, 'The beer went mad.' A heroin addict, explaining his resort to the needle will say, 'Heroin's everywhere.' It is as if the beer drank the alcoholic and the heroin injected the addict. (ix)

Dalrymple's most expressive example for the form of passive speech adopted by those who refuse to accept responsibility for their acts and thereby reject the idea of free will is the explanation given by one murderer: *the knife went in* (2001: 6).

Here, Dalrymple is clearly speaking about a specific variety of language, a diction or form of speech which is common to the underclass in urban Britain with which he works. The diction and grammar of members of the underclass not only reflects the way they think, according to Dalrymple, it determines the way they act and therefore forges their ultimate social destiny. Unless they can break out of this fatalistic condition of shrugging responsibility, unless they can assume both grammatically and morally the active form in their choice of verbs and in their choice of actions, they are doomed to remain within the grip of the poverty trap, Dalrymple argues.

A similar use of the term *language* (though one found in very different circles) would be to claim that a poet's language teaches us to understand our feelings by giving an expression to them.

Schiller spoke of a cultivated language that *poetises* and *thinks for* you (Klemperer 1975: 26). For Schiller and Dalrymple, the degree to which we use language lucidly and sensitively reflects our understanding of the world and our place within it.

Their use of *language* is clearly different from the one found in the following claim about worldviews made by Marianne Mithun:

> The loss of a language represents a definitive separation of a people from its heritage. It also represents an irreparable loss for us all, the loss of opportunities to glimpse alternative ways of making sense of the human experience. (quoted in Dalby 2003: 253)

Mithun obviously has in mind languages of different linguistic communities or nations; in this instance, endangered or dying languages. This fact is made clear by the context.

But the context does not always allow us to ascertain the exact meaning of the term, and sometimes multiple interpretations become possible. Wittgenstein is often quoted for his famous line from the *Tractatus Logico-Philosophicus* (Wittgenstein 1969b: proposition 5.6, p. 64), which translates as: 'The limits of my language mean the limits of my world.' But what did Wittgenstein mean exactly by '*Die Grenzen meiner Sprache* bedeuten die Grenze meiner Welt?' (italics in the German text, 1984: 67). Did he mean German as a language, or his own personal knowledge of the language? Could he reach beyond the limits he spoke of by extending his knowledge of his mother tongue? Or would he, like Whorf suggested, need to reach into the thought world of a radically different language, such as Hopi or Korean? Indeed, in Wittgenstein's sentence, all three terms, *Sprache*, *Welt* and *bedeuten* (translated above as *mean*, though it can also designate *define*) are open to interpretation.

Does the language we are born into limit and define the world or does it open up the world to us? To what extent does the world of which we speak correspond to the world that exists in and of itself? As someone intrigued by the capacity of language to generate truth claims about the world, Wittgenstein, no doubt had language's capacity to enable us to speak of reality in mind. Nevertheless, the sentence has passed into English as a famous quote and takes on different interpretations in different places. This is not the place to plunge into Wittgenstein's investigations or their repercussions for debates about language in English-speaking countries. It is simply a question of stressing the usefulness of avoiding ambiguity when speaking about the way language expresses ideas and helps us to refine them. Though many scholars may agree that language shapes or influences thought, some will have in mind the language system, others will have in mind the way in which individual speakers use the language system, and relatively few thinkers will, like Humboldt, clearly define the interaction between the language's influence on individual expression and the contribution of that individual expression to the ongoing development of the language system.

THOUGHT

The verb *to think* is a curious catch-all term, and this is true of its equivalent terms in French (*penser*), in German (*denken*), and in Czech (*mýslet*). The term in English enfolds a wide variety of meanings:

- to exercise the mind
- to resolve ideas in the mind
- to judge, or be of the opinion
- to consider
- to conceive or hit upon an idea
- to imagine
- to believe
- to expect
- to purpose, or design.

Often the meaning of the verb *to think* coincides with (or overlaps) the meanings of more specialised forms of conscious and unconscious thought designated by the following verbs:

- to perceive
- to feel

- to contemplate
- to analyse
- to criticise
- to evaluate
- to reason.

Often the very distinction between conscious and unconscious thought will become problematic (which perhaps explains why the term *semi-conscious* has been found so useful). To what extent is perception conscious? Can we contemplate something without *thinking*, if we mean by the latter, analysing and reasoning? It is true that we are often advised to avoid such self-conscious forms of thought when appreciating art, music or poetry. We can will ourselves into a more intense form of awareness, a contemplation of a religious or meditative kind. Prayer as well as Zen and Tao philosophies encourage us to cultivate such a form of awareness. To what extent is such an awareness *unthinking* or *unconscious*? It would perhaps be a mistake to try to fit such forms of thought or *spiritual presence* into the binary opposition *conscious/unconscious*.

Feeling would seem to be at the opposite end of reasoning, or so it has been situated since the Romantics began criticising the Enlightenment. But to what extent is feeling *unconscious*? Are pain, pleasure, love and aversion not experiences which well up within us and fill our consciousness?

This is not the place to attempt a definition of consciousness, but for our discussion of the relationship between language and worldview, it is essential to distinguish between different forms of thought and to establish whether language acts upon them, and if so, in what ways. Making such distinctions will allow us not simply to avoid contention, but also to avoid something much more pernicious to our study, unfounded agreement. As we saw at the opening of this book, many linguists and philosophers admit that thought is influenced by language, but since the terms of the discussion are ill-defined, fluctuating and, all too often, misconstrued, those who admit the influence often seem to be agreeing to very different ideas. Crystal, Stamm, Whorf, Sapir, Humboldt and Trabant would all agree that language and thought are related, but it will be impossible to establish whether these thinkers share a common understanding of the relationship between the two until we have first defined what they mean by both *thought* and *language*.

Crystal, for example, makes it clear that he feels that language can influence rational, directed logical and propositional thinking (1997: 14). Humboldt argues that language is active at a far more fundamental level than this, however. He believes that it is essential to the process of conceptualisation. Whorf and Sapir respectively suggest that language provides *ruts* or *grooves* within which, or along which, we think. Such a patterning would seem to suggest an influence on both conscious and unconscious thought, though Sapir (like Humboldt) was careful to point out that the active individual mind was in no way imprisoned in language and could work upon it. Both, Sapir and Humboldt, furthermore, resisted or refused the idea of the mind as an object which was worked upon by language (conceived as an active subject).

Curiously, Crystal admits that language 'does influence the way we perceive and remember', and that 'it affects the way we perform mental tasks' (1997: 15). So he obviously does not restrict language's influence to the intellectual activity of the conscious mind. But, he begins the sentence just quoted with the words, 'Language may not determine the way we think . . .' (ibid.). Unfortunately, Crystal does not define what kind of 'thinking' he has in mind here. We can only conjecture on this point: he seems to be resisting a deterministic model of language in which the active power of language would imprison thought. Man, for Crystal, must be free, and indeed the impression of freedom is one we all share. Each of us feels ourself free to express what we feel as we feel it when we speak.

At this point it becomes clear how crucial a step was taken by Humboldt (and to a lesser extent Sapir) when he insisted that language was the work of individuals handed down to individuals. For Humboldt, thought gives form to itself in language, and the thought of individuals is taken on and reshaped by individuals for their own usage as they express themselves within language's frameworks by using its classifications and concepts. Our thought will run smoothly along well-worn grooves, but this does not prevent us from striking out of those grooves or tracing new lines to refine language as a mode of expression.

This is clear in the way we redefine our categories and definitions in language. A language which has no distinction between apes and monkeys (as French initially did not) can invent one (*singe/grand singe*). The landlocked language, Czech, seems initially to have defined the whale (*velryba*) in a similar manner: the morphology clearly categorises it as a sub-species of fish (*ryba*) of an enormous size (*vel* from *velký*, meaning great). But obviously, this does not prevent all Czechs from realising that a whale is a mammal.

Our categories are often revised and refined by thought and the way we conceive things cannot be considered to be rigidly limited by language (though we might find it easier to define things when suitable distinctions are readily available). English, for example, offers a distinction between *purple* and *violet*, where French uses only one term *violet*. This may make us more sensitive to different shades of the colour. However, a visit to any decorating or DIY store throughout the world will suffice to remind us that all languages can invent a multitude of distinctions between different colours and shades when they are required. We will find on the shelves of the paint section, for example, *burnt ochre orange* and *deep sky blue* just as their equivalents in French, German or Czech can be found. In this sense, rather than imprisoning the mind, language offers it patterns with which to think. And part of the process of thinking with patterns becomes the exploration of extended patterns and the invention of alternative patterns of thought.

WORLDVIEW

Certain objections have already been made to the term *worldview*. It has been used to imply a fixed conception of the world which envelops the thinking subject. It also highlights the visual aspect of perception while downplaying other forms of knowing the world. For this reason, I have already suggested we redefine our terms.

In place of worldview-as-*Weltansicht*, I propose the following distinction:

- *world-perceiving*, for the changing and developing perception we have of the world,

- *world-conceiving*, for the changing and developing manner in which we draw that world into the realm of thought and form concepts and frameworks to represent things and our experience of the world.

This distinction should enable us to highlight both the pre-conscious organising process which directs to some extent the way we perceive the world and the cognitive activity of organising the world we perceive through our senses. Though this distinction replaces a single term in Humboldt's thought, it is clear from his writings that what he meant by *Weltansicht* involved both processes.

In place of worldview-as-*Weltanschauung*, I propose three terms:

- *Cultural mindset* for that relatively rigid and fixed conception of the world which frames our perception and conception of politics, society, history, behaviour, the individual's place in the world and the organising frameworks of social relations. When groups and generations fail to understand each other though they 'speak the same language', it is because their cultural mindsets have grown into very different expressions of the world though those expressions are derived from the same world-perceiving and world-conceiving which organise the language shared by all groups within their linguistic community.
- *Personal world* for the perception and conception of the world which is specific to each individual. This designates the individual's own form or version of the mindset he or she adheres to both consciously and unconsciously.
- *Perspective* for the changing nature of the way each person perceives and conceives the world. An individual's perspective changes as he or she moves through the world, interacting with others and encountering new and different experiences. Perspective is active, or rather interactive, and that is why it is constantly changing. Just as the changing nature of the world to some extent fashions the perspective we have of that world, so the way we ourselves change as we adopt new ideas and expressions with age and experience, in turn (and simultaneously) alters the way we perceive the world.

These five terms, world-perceiving, world-conceiving, cultural mindset, personal world and perspective, are merely proposals. They should serve primarily to highlight the concepts that are hidden by the single term worldview. These terms are distinctions not classifications. That is to say, one concept does not exclude another: quite the opposite is true. A man's perspective constitutes the present disposition of his personal world, which itself forms part of a cultural mindset. Though the cultural mindset is fixed to a certain extent, this should not obscure the fact that it is continually developing as the language we speak is modified by the speech of men and women. The cultural mindset in turn is only one possible form of world-perceiving and world-conceiving.

It may be useful to illustrate the relationship between these five concepts as circles within circles in which world-perceiving ripples out towards perspective.

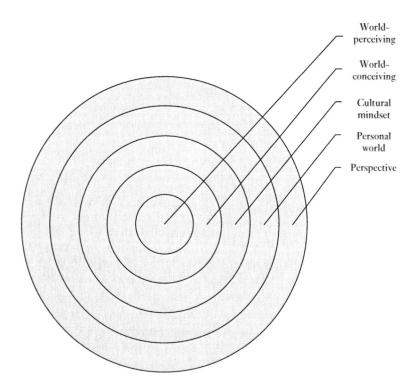

World-
perceiving

World-
conceiving

Cultural
mindset

Personal
world

Perspective

This paradigm should not, however, induce us to imagine that the ripples always spread outwards from world-conceiving within the language to each individual's changing perspective. To believe this would be a gross misinterpretation of Humboldt's linguistic philosophy. If Humboldt's thought can be described as linguistic anthropology, it is because he places the individual – or rather individuals – at the centre of language. It is not only perfectly legitimate to assume that an individual's perspective contributes to the retracing of the contours of world-perceiving: this is, in fact, the only imaginable origin of world-perceiving. Language is handed down to individuals from other individuals and it is the combined interaction between those individuals in speech which reanimates and reshapes the living language.

This may have gone someway to clarifying the concept of world-view, but the history of the term deserves some further consideration before we can start afresh to understand language using a new *purified* taxonomy. The term worldview has a haunting past that must be exorcised. *Worldview* has, at times, been used as an *anti-idea*. By this I mean that the term worldview has been used to refuse or refute other alternative belief systems by those who assert that their own worldview transcends such belief systems. Worldview, in this usage of the term, comes to mean the one true conception of the world in a world full of misconceptions. The one worldview, it is believed, anchors itself in experience of reality, while other belief systems have lost their moorings.

Ironically, *worldview* is often used as an *anti-idea* by those who wish to impose their own ideology by discrediting the very idea of ideology. This is perhaps the most pernicious and perverted use of the term. Klemperer, in his study of *Nazi-speak* (*LTI*) gave the term's usage careful consideration. He was surprised to see the way the usage of *Weltanschauung* had changed radically in German from the beginning of the twentieth century and the mid-1930s.

As we have already seen, at the beginning of the century its usage had been restricted to intellectuals of a neo-Romantic bent. Paradoxically, the members of the Nazi party who began to give the term a wider usage were reacting directly against the ideas of the neo-Romantics when they denounced their decadence, their impressionism, their scepticism and their idea of the disintegration of the fixed ego of experience. This did not prevent the Nazi party from concocting their own mixture of neo-Romantic metaphysical jargon, however, which they proceeded to fuse with their down-to-earth anti-intellectualism. The popularisation of the term *Weltanschauung* coincided with the introduction of a muggy metaphysics into diverse fields of everyday life. For example, party doctrine advocated the 'dedication to the convictions of the interior of infinity', by which the party seemed to imply something that was supposed to be both comprehensible for, and applicable to, each and everyone. In a similar act of linguistic obfuscation, insurance payments (*Versicherungsprämien*), were renamed 'contributions to a worldview community' (*Beiträge zu einer weltanschaulichen Gemeinschaft*, Klemperer 1975: 186).

Weltanschauung, in the Nazi usage of the term, reveals a latent anti-intellectualism in the term which the Nazis were able to exploit so efficiently. For the Romantics, the term was useful in that it resisted the reduction of experience, thought and feeling to Reason. But the *radiant worldview* the Nazis were promoting was not so much hostile to the reduction of experience, thought and feeling to Reason as it was hostile to thought and reason themselves. Thought and reason represented a menace to the Nazi party because they could be used to demand that the Nazis defend their doctrine. Since the party's popularity was largely based not upon reason, or reasoned thought, or even upon a coherent ideological conception of man, society and history (as communist ideology arguably was), but rather upon irrational impulses such as hate, resentment, frustrated patriotism and a desire to serve, any reasoned discussion of the party would only serve to reveal its irrationality.

The affection the Nazis felt for the term *Weltanschauung* can also be explained partly by the fact that it was (in contrast to *ideology*) a term which sprang from German roots. It therefore seemed to correspond better to the German spirit. This was a period in which it became very fashionable to *Germanise* foreign words in order to pretend that what was imported lexically had in fact sprung from the soil of the German language (Klemperer 1975). It must be said, however, that this was more a fashion than a policy and the Nazi Party, which was eager to appear both modern and cultivated, did even at times denounce this aversion to foreign terms.

The passion for Germanising words and avoiding foreign-sounding concepts (*Fremdwörter*) seems to have contributed to the popularisation of the hitherto intellectual term *Weltanschauung*, nonetheless: but the charm of the concept lay as much in what it did not mean as in what it meant. *Weltanschauung* was not *a philosophy*. *Weltanschauung* was superior to philosophy not only because it was a German word, not a Greek one. It was also superior because it struck its roots into something within both the German soul and the German tradition, and it promised to body forth, in Nazi aspirations, something more immediate and fundamental than an intellectual concept such as *philosophy* ever could.

Nazi ideology set itself in opposition to logic and reason (the modes of philosophical thought), and offered as their alternative, *the right-way of seeing things* (*das richtige Sehen*, Klemperer 1975: 187; 2006: 135). This was something that every party member could respond to. For Nazis, philosophy was foreign, Marxism was 'Jewish': both would weaken the strong German soul, if they were allowed to survive. And the conviction instilled in the party member by his worldview (a perception which was both deeply personal and deeply shared with other party members) fuelled his self-righteous sense of indignation when confronted with intellectuals whose ideas escaped him. While remaining very graspable and palpable as an idea, *Weltanschauung* simultaneously promised, over and above philosophy, access to an almost spiritual insight into things. With the idea of vision (*Schau*), Klemperer explains, the language of the Nazi party exploited the idea of a mystical form of Vision, the sight of the inner-eye, the intuition and the revelation of religious ecstasy. In the Nazi use of the term *Weltanschauung*, Klemperer found some remnant of the neo-Romantics' nostalgia for the vision of the Redeemer from whom the vital living principle of our world shines forth (ibid.). Klemperer went on to demonstrate the way the Nazis exploited this idea of vision (*Schau*) in another way, linking it to a Hollywood-inspired concept of *show*. The director of Nazi propaganda, Goebbels, notably, seems to have cherished the fusion of the religious with the Hollywoodesque in the enraptured rhetoric of his rallies. This short summary should suffice to prove that the concept *worldview* has not always been used with the most innocent of intentions.

In a much less radical (but no less fundamental) fashion, many of the recent publications in English in which the term *worldview* is used reflect a desire to avoid such words as philosophy and ideology. In general, any system of beliefs which wishes to rise above the status of one system of beliefs among others will try to elevate its worldview to the status of Truth (and in doing so will often avoid the term *belief* itself). The fast-growing Christian scholarship which has latched onto the term *worldview* and whose main exponents are Naugle (2002) and Sire (2004), certainly seem to defend something which should be held to be more fundamental than Reason and something which transcends ideology when they use the term.

Naugle tries to transplant *worldview* into the framework of Christian thought, notably by linking it to the notion of the *heart*. His insistence on the importance of the human *heart* as a concept is both traditional, in that it reactivates an ancient Biblical metaphor, and radical, in that it is through the use of *heart* that Naugle hopes to harness *worldview* as a Christian concept. In this, Naugle has his work cut out. He poses the question in the following manner:

> To what extent does worldview as a modernist concept not only carry the connotation of relativism, but paradoxically also convey a thoroughgoing objectification which is equally antithetical to an historic, Christian understanding of creation and humankind and the relationship between them? (2002: 331)

Ultimately, Naugle seeks to oppose the relativism implicit in the term worldview, especially the existentialist relativism of the German philosopher, Karl Jaspers, who in 1919 wrote his *Psychologie der Weltanschauungen* (which unfortunately has never been translated into English). In his concluding chapter, Naugle recognises that there is an implicit danger in the term worldview (a tripartite philosophical, theoretical and spiritual danger), but he sees the term as a challenge that Christian thought must take on and answer. He formulates three reasons for this:

The first is that worldview has played an extraordinary role in modern and Christian thought. The second is that it is one of the central intellectual conceptions in recent times. The third is that it is a notion of utmost, if not final, human, cultural, and Christian significance. (2002: 344)

But if *worldview* as a concept is unavoidable for Naugle, a philosopher or a political thinker would probably argue that in his use of the term to discuss the individual's relationship to society, he is avoiding using other terms, namely *philosophy* and *ideology*. For Marx, the refusal to take an ideological perspective and the belief that you can lift yourself above ideology, are in themselves ideological acts. Can the Church escape entanglement in social, political, ideological and philosophical questions? Is the use of worldview an attempt to reformulate a spiritual presence in the world that transcends alternative formulations? If so, such an attempt will be met by many with scepticism. The church's *apolitical* stance has all too often been revealed to be highly political. Christianity has often been equated with conservatism. The Catholic Church has often been accused of refusing to take a stance on essential and urgent political questions. The refusal to take a stance is, ultimately, in itself is a political act. In this way, the use of *worldview* by Christians may be construed as a political attempt to depoliticise our conception of society.

The very popularity of the term *worldview*, and the fact that so many different people at different times have found the term useful for expressing a very personal, individual, but also fundamental and often shared vision of reality, should make us wary of adopting the term. If no word is innocent, then worldview is steeped in multiple traditions, and often it is the hue of this or that tradition which makes the term attractive to its users. Whether we unwittingly adopt aspects of a tradition (as those inclined towards cultural relativism often do when they adopt the term worldview), whether we adopt aspects of the term and adapt them to our own ends (as the Nazis did in adapting the neo-Romantic critique of Reason that was associated with the German term *Weltanschauung*), or whether we adopt the term and resist traditions which have developed around it and left their imprint upon it (as Naugle resists the relativistic existentialist use of the term *Weltanschauung* which has coloured our notion of *worldview*), the term remains problematic, controversial and ambiguous.

But worst of all, the term permits diverse people with opposed ideas to fall under the spell of believing they agree with one another. Goebbels, as the arch-demagogue of Nazi-party rhetoric, was no doubt amused at how successful his party propaganda was in convincing the masses that they shared the same ideals as the party's leaders, but Goebbels' and Hitler's writings make it perfectly plain that they intended propaganda to be a tool to be used to manipulate the gullible masses who would always be more easily convinced by a big lie than by a small one. It seems probable, then, that even in promoting the *radiant Weltanschauung*, there was one worldview for the masses, who could identify with the aims of the party in a direct and personal fashion, and another for the visionaries of the *Weltanschauung*.

It is partly to relieve our shoulders of the heavy heritage of the term *Weltanschauung*, that I have opted for using the five terms introduced above: *world-perceiving*, *world-conceiving*, *cultural mindset*, *personal world* and *perspective*. Now we have, as it were, disinfected the term *worldview*, these terms should clarify the various concepts it covers. These terms should help refocus the debate concerning the relationship between language and thought upon the conception of language left to us by Humboldt.

Like *worldview*, these terms can be used to describe the varying degrees of individuality in language that lie between the creative use of speech made by the individual speaker and the shared conception of a nation or linguistic community as it is fashioned and refashioned in speech. Though Humboldt always stressed the personal and subjective aspect of speech, and though this aspect of his thought has been preserved in the relativistic use of the term *Weltanschauung*, Chomsky, Langham Brown and Losonsky were not mistaken in highlighting the fact that Humboldt was interested in working towards something that went beyond individual speech: linguistic universals. Humboldt, in comparing the infinite variety of linguistic constructs, was equally eager to define the constants to be found in the flux of speech: he was interested in defining the ways in which individual human attempts combined within different languages to express something of the truth of our shared world. In this, he was very different from Jaspers, who posited the relative nature or worldviews and from linguists like Whorf who felt some languages were better than others for expressing the experience of a linguistic community. While Humboldt clearly felt that languages explore the various facets of reality with greater or lesser delicacy and sophistication, he avoids setting up hierarchies by which to classify superior and inferior languages. For Humboldt, perception, conception, experience and expression were all bound up together in one evolving, ongoing struggle of individual minds to formulate what they thought and felt.

CHAPTER 16

A Final Word

Those who seek simple classifications for things will perhaps be disappointed with this short study of worldview which has led us back through Whorf, Sapir and Boas to discover something of Humboldt's linguistic philosophy. Simple classifications might be useful when we are dealing with simple things. But for Humboldt, language is not made up of things: objects to be explored and catalogued. Nor was he enamoured of classifications. If he was wary of them, it was because classifications are so often used to pigeonhole languages. As such, divisions and dissections will more likely deform our perception of the living activity of speech as it is distilled in language. Each language is a complex developing system, the vibrant synthesis of almost infinite individual expression. As such, it will always defy exhaustive description. Classifications offer not conceptions but misconceptions, if they deceive us into believing that we can rise above language to circumscribe the limits of different languages and compare them with some omniscient, supra-linguistic intelligence. God may be able to do so, but men and women live and breathe and think within language: within a specific language system. We may be able to intuit something of a foreign language's incommensurate difference which contrasts with our own mode of thought, but the belief that we can pin that difference down is pure folly. And the desire to pin it down betrays the fact that we have transformed speech (the dynamic interactive force which binds people together in time and space) into a model of language perceived as a static object, an object of scientific study.

Our short study of worldview has taken us on a tour of ideas concerning language, a tour that has been critical in its approach. Yet, it is not a question of rejecting the authors in question, but rather of grappling with the definitions they provide and with the expressions they give to the relationship between thought and language. The curiosity which animated Sapir and Whorf led them to form insights and give expression to intuitions of great sensitivity. And yet, the Anglo-American tradition proved insufficient for formulating a totally convincing model of worldview. From Sapir and Whorf, we were led back to the German philological tradition to unearth Humboldt's linguistic anthropology and to explore Trabant's distinction between Humboldt's concept of *Weltansicht* and the more commonly used term *Weltanschauung*.

However, this distinction for obvious linguistic reasons cannot be imported directly into English and even the two terms prove problematic since the latter has become the repository of contradictory meanings (some of which are politically disreputable). Moreover, linguists persistently associate worldview in English with *Weltanschauung* and for the most part are entirely ignorant of the concept of *Weltansicht*. In order to extricate the key concept of worldview from confusion, and in order to highlight the importance of forms of sensory perception other than that of sight, five fresh concepts have been proposed in place of worldview: world-perceiving, world-conceiving, cultural mindset, personal world and perspective.

These are distinctions, not classifications. And their status is of a purely speculative nature. If they help us to clarify our thought about the various concepts that have been designated by the term *worldview*, then they will be of some value in helping us to debate the nature of language with greater sensitivity and precision.

To return to the crucial and urgent question of the ecolinguists, the saving of endangered languages and the safeguarding of worldviews radically different from our own, these distinctions may (it is hoped) allow us to discern with ruthlessly unromantic empirical eyes something fundamental in the specific way each language cultivates (and is cultivated by) its linguistic community. If these distinctions fail to allow us to do this, if they fail to help us to express more clearly the way we perceive, understand and express our experience of the world, then they will be rightfully modified or discarded.

Though speech in many ways transcends the utilitarian model of language-use, philosophical and analytical discourse still requires *conceptual tools*. If, by investigating the thought of Wilhelm von Humboldt, we have been able to hone our tools, our exploration of language and reality may make us more perceptive and lucid as we carve our way through words towards expression.

Glossary

Cultural mindset Term used in this work to designate that relatively rigid and fixed way of seeing the world which frames our perception and conception of politics, society, history, behaviour, the individual's place in the world and the organising conceptual frameworks of social relations. When groups and generations who speak the same language fail to understand each other, it is because their cultural mindsets have grown into very different expressions of the world though those differing expressions are derived from the same world-perceiving and world-conceiving which organise the language shared by all groups within their linguistic community.

Ecolinguistics A discipline practised by a group of radical linguists, including Hagège in France and Crystal in the English-speaking world, who have been militating since the 1980s to safeguard dying and endangered languages in order to preserve what these linguists claim to be the essential specificity of each language as an expression of the world.

Ethnolinguistics In English-speaking linguistics this term is a synonym for **linguistic anthropology**.

Form In Humboldt's thought, the patterns which, through the mind's struggle towards expression in language, come to *form* enduring and reusable channels and constellations of meaning.

Language system Term used in this work to designate the language of a linguistic community, e.g. English, French, Portuguese or Wolof. This term has been used to distinguish it from alternative definitions of *language* such as the one referred to when we speak of the stylistic effects and diction characteristic of a certain writer's language, for example.

Linguistic anthropology In the English-speaking academic community, linguistic anthropology is concerned with the study of language as one essential aspect of anthropology as a whole. Given that modern linguistics has often chosen to privilege the study of language structure and formal detail at the expense of meaning within the social context, linguistic anthropology has taken on the task of compensating for this partial blindness by studying the use of speech and the relationship between language and culture. Man, as a social animal, is a linguistic animal for this approach. It should be clear from this short summary that linguistic anthropology as it is practised in the US has derived from the mother-discipline, anthropology. It therefore differs fundamentally from what has come in recent decades to be called in France *l'anthropologie linguistique*. The latter school of scholarship has its roots in philology and is inspired by Humboldt's approach to language. For Meschonnic and Trabant (its main exponents), linguistic anthropology should be reserved for the study of the individual from the perspective of his or her expression in language. Central to their work is the interpretation of the way the individual defines him- of herself as a linguistic subject in relation to others in the act of speaking. While linguistic anthropology as it is practised in the English-speaking world might be considered a synonym of *ethnolinguistics*, Meschonnic's work might be considered to be closer to our disciplines of discourse analysis and stylistics, though since schools of thought do not travel along identical trajectories, the term *anthropologie linguistique* defies translation to some extent.

Linguistic relativity hypothesis Term associated with Whorf and Sapir among English-speaking linguists such as John A. Lucy, Zdenek Salzmann and David Crystal. For Whorf, all languages are thought worlds impenetrable to the thought of those who speak another language. The thought world, as Whorf expounds the term, does at times appear to entail a series of constraints which limit thought, but Whorf did envisage a certain give and take between language and culture. The thought world embraced both language and culture and the interaction between the two, in his conception of language. The more 'exotic' the language, the greater the divide between its modes of patterning for thought and expression and those of our own. Consequently the more effort we must make when we enter into this exotic thought world to strive to assimilate its patterns and conceptual categories into our own consciousness when we adopt it as a second language. For Sapir, different languages were different systems of thought, infinitely complex and intricate configurations of patterning, which were formed by living speech as expression solidifies into what might be considered the sediment of our language. For Sapir, these systems were incommensurable. Each language system channels the thought of its speakers along familiar lines. Since these lines or 'grooves' were different in kind, for Sapir, it followed that thought was in some respects 'relative'. If thought is language-bound and language-dependent, the fundamental differences between languages (we are forced to conclude) will incline us to formulate differently the way we experience and express the world around us. Sapir did not see the individual as a slave of language, imprisoned within its concepts and grammatical constraints: on the contrary he was fascinated by original creative expression and by what makes each person's speech the reflection of his or her personality. But he did see free, self-liberating, expression and creativity in language as something which took conventional speech as its starting point. The innovative speaker reflects upon common usage within the configurations of thought which language itself opens up to us. Linguistic relativity for him, was defined as '. . . a kind of relativity that is generally hidden from us by our naïve acceptance of fixed habits of speech as guides to an objective understanding of the nature of experience. This is the relativity of concepts or, as it might be called, the relativity of the form of thought' (Sapir, quoted by Lucy 1996: 20–1).

Personal world Term used in this work to designate the perception and conception of the world which is specific to each individual. This *personal world* constitutes the individual's own form or version of the mindset he or she adheres to both consciously and unconsciously. Though this world constitutes a stance and as such it may change over time, the personal world remains within the life and personality of the individual to a certain degree coherent and regular (habitual if not constant). In contrast to this, his or her perspective changes with circumstances and interaction with others.

Perspective Term used in this work to designate the changing nature of the way each individual perceives and conceives the world. An individual's *perspective* changes as he or she moves through the world, interacting with others and discovering new and different experiences. *Perspective* is active, or rather interactive, and for that reason it is constantly changing. Just as the changing nature of the world to some extent fashions the perspective we have of it, so the way we ourselves change (adopting new ideas and expressions with age and experience) alters the way we perceive the world.

Subjectivation Term coined in French by Henri Meschonnic (and introduced into English in this book). *Subjectivation* designates the creative reformulation of language by a speaking or writing subject who, in the act of harnessing language to give expression to his or her ideas, thereby defines him- or herself as a linguistic subject (the *I* of discourse). Meschonnic embraces Humboldt's idea of the subjective transformation of language and, like him, stresses the importance of literature for language. Like Humboldt, Meschonnic believes that language outside of individual expression does not exist and that the language system can only survive thanks to its ongoing reformulation within the discourse of individuals, the discourse within which the *I* is bodied forth as a subject among subjects. Meschonnic is arguably more a thinker inspired by Humboldt than a Humboldt scholar, in that his prolific *oeuvre* over the last three decades has tended to further Humboldt's thought by exploring his intuition that literature can quicken the spirit of language, give life to it and reanimate it when the expressive potential of language dulls through uninspired usage, unreflective repetition or overuse. *Subjectivation* is one of the concepts Meschonnic uses to designate the process by which language is always inspired and kept alive by individual expression, an individual expression which transforms language by reorganising the relations between words. Of particular interest to Meschonnic is the highly individual or specific way a poet treats word-play, rhyme, accentuation and line breaks for example. Though traditionally versification has tended to treat some of these questions as formal ones, Meschonnic joins Humboldt and Sapir in stressing the semantic consequences of what have been reduced to formal flourishes in language. *Subjectivation* is interesting as a concept in that it neatly reminds us that all expression in speech is subjective and that all language which is offered up as the raw material for expression is initially and ultimately subjective in origin and nature. In this sense, the term *subjectivation* should serve in both French and English to shake us out of formalist, abstract or depersonalised representations of speech and language which inevitably tend to pervert our perception of the way we communicate.

Thought world Term used by Whorf to designate the way a culture understands the universe. Though *thought world* is at times expressed as *Weltanschauug* in Whorf's thought, it seems clear that what he has in mind when he uses both terms is closer to Humboldt's concept of *Weltansicht*.

Weltanschauung In Trabant's *Weltansicht–Weltanschauung* distinction inspired by Humboldt, the vision of the world, mindset or ideology which language allows people to develop for themselves to help them understand the world, what is in it and their own place within that world. A *Weltanschauung* constitutes an individual's or a community's interpretation of the world or the interpretative framework which he or she invokes to help understand the world. In contrast, the *Weltansicht* inherent in a language offers the world up to us for interpretation by allowing us to form concepts and exchange ideas about those concepts and the relationships between them. While *Weltansichten* affirm nothing about the world, *Weltanschauungen* can be regarded as belief systems, hypotheses about the way the world really *is*. For this reason, *Weltanschauung* is often felt to be closely related to *ideology*. It should, nevertheless, be stressed that though Humboldt was Ambassador for Prussia in a period of war and exercised a high political office, he did not seek to advance political ideas in his linguistic philosophy.

Weltansicht In Trabant's *Weltansicht–Weltanschauung* distinction inspired by Humboldt, the capacity which language endows us with to form the concepts with which we think and which we need in order to communicate. While the *Weltansicht* of a language is implicit to it and inseparable from it, *Weltanschauungen* are not dependent upon the language system in which they are found. Several contradictory *Weltanschauungen* can exist within the same language, and they can migrate between radically different language systems. Religious and political worldviews which spread throughout the world taking root in different cultures testify amply to the truth of the fact that *Weltanschauungen* are not language-bound.

Work of the mind The mental activity of negotiating with and in language in order to express ideas. While the mind can accept the form of language as adequate to its needs for expression, it can also innovate while using given concepts, channels and constellations of meaning. A third option remains open to the mind, however: it can refuse both existing patterns of thought and the temptation to adapt them, by striking out in an entirely new direction.

World-conceiving Term used in this work to designate one aspect of Humboldt's concept of *Weltansicht*, namely the changing and developing manner in which we draw that world into the realm of thought to form concepts and frameworks to represent things and our experience of the world.

World-perceiving Term used in this work to denote one aspect of Humboldt's concept of *Weltansicht*, namely the changing and developing perception we have of the world.

Worldview Since the aim of this whole work is to redefine *worldview*, it is somewhat perverse to attempt to encapsulate all of the complexities and contradictions which this sole term has come to include. However, since the term has gained wide currency in the disciplines of philosophy, sociology and cultural studies as well as in linguistics, and since it is not likely to be discarded, some attempt should be made to define it. Though any attempt at definition will be inadequate, it seems, nevertheless, reasonable to affirm that this catch-all term covers five different concepts which I have attempted to disentangle using the terms *world-perceiving*, *world-conceiving*, *cultural mindset*, *personal world* and *perspective* as defined above.

Bibliography

Adorno, Theodor W. (1991), *Notes to Literature*, ed. Rolf Tiedemann, trans. Shierry Weber Nicholsen, New York: Columbia University Press.

Auroux, Sylvain (1996), *La philosophie du langage*, Paris: Presses Universitaires de France.

Berlin, Isaiah (2000), *Three Critics of the Enlightenment: Vico, Hamann, Herder*, Princeton, NJ: Princeton University Press.

Boas, Franz [1911] (1973), *Introduction to Handbook of American Indian Languages*, Lincoln: Nebraska University Press.

Chabrolle-Cerretini, Anne-Marie (2007), *La vision du monde de Wilhelm von Humboldt: Histoire d'un concept linguistique*, Lyon: ENS Éditions.

Chomsky, Noam (1972), *Language and Mind*, enlarged edition, New York: Harcourt Brace.

Copleston, Frederick S. J. (1962), *A History of Western Philosophy, in 9 volumes*, New York: Image Books.

Crystal, David (2000), *Language Death*, Cambridge: Cambridge University Press.

Crystal, David (1997), *The Cambridge Encyclopaedia of Language*, 2nd edn, Cambridge: Cambridge University Press.

Crystal, David [1997] (2003), *English as a Global Language*, 2nd edn, Cambridge: Cambridge University Press.

Dalby, Andrew (2003), *Language in Danger*, London: Penguin.

Dalrymple, Theodore (2001), *Life at the Bottom: The Worldview that Makes the Underclass*, Chicago: Ivan R. Dee.

de Certeau, Michel, Dominique Julia and Jacques Revel (1975), *Une politique de la langue: La révolution française et les patois: l'enquête de Grégoire*, Paris: Gallimard.

Ducrot, Oswald and Jean-Marie Schaeffer (1995), *Nouveau dictionnaire encyclopédique des sciences du langage*, Paris: Seuil.

Dubois, Jean, Mathée Giacomo, Louis Guespin, Christianne Marcellesi, Jean-Baptiste Marcellesi and Jean-Pierre Mével (1994), *Dictionnaire de linguistique et des sciences du langage*, Paris: Larousse.

Eckermann, Johann Peter [1835] (1982), *Gespräche mit Goethe in den letzten Jahren seines Lebens*, Berlin and Weimar: Aufbau-Verlag.

Eckermann, Johann Peter (1998), *Conversations with Goethe*, trans. John Oxenford, ed. J. K. Moorhead, New York: Da Capo Press.

Eliot, T. S. (1953), *Selected Prose*, London: Penguin.

Eliot, T. S. (1969), *Complete Poems and Plays*, London: Faber and Faber.

Flew, Antony (1979), *A Dictionary of Philosophy*, London: Pan Books/Macmillan Press.

Guillemin-Flescher, Jacqueline (1981), *Syntaxe comparée du français et de l'anglais: problèmes de traduction*, Paris: Ophrys.

Hagège, Claude (1985), *L'homme de paroles: Contribution linguistique aux sciences humaines*, Paris: Fayard.

Hagège, Claude (2000), *Le Souffle de la langue*, Paris: Odile Jacob.

Hagège, Claude [2000] (2002), *Halte à la mort des langues*, Paris: Odile Jacob.

Hansen-Løve, Ole (1972), *La révolution copernicienne du langage dans l'oeuvre de Wilhelm von Humboldt*, Paris: Varia.

Humboldt, Wilhelm von [1836] (1971), *Linguistic Variability and Intellectual Development*, trans. George C. Buck and Frithjof A. Raven, Philadelphia: Pennsylvania University Press.

Humboldt, Wilhelm von [1836] (1999), *On language: On the Diversity of Human Language Construction and its Influence on the Mental Development of the Human Species*, trans. Peter Heath and ed. Michael Losonsky, Cambridge: Cambridge University Press.

Humboldt, Wilhelm von (2000), *Sur le caractère national des langues et autres écrits sur le langage*, presented, translated and with commentary by Denis Thouard, Paris: Seuil.

Humboldt, Wilhelm von [1836] (2003), *Über die Verschiedenheit des menschlichen Sprachbaues/ Über die Sprache*, Berlin: Fourier Verlag.

Jaspers, Karl (1962), *Plato and Augustine*, trans. from German by Ralph Manheim, ed. Hannah Arendt, New York: Harcourt Brace Jovanovich.

Klemperer, Victor [1957] (1975), *LTI: Notizbuch eines Philologen*, Leipzig: Reclam Verlag.

Klemperer, Victor (1996), *LTI: la langue du IIIe Reich*, trans. from German with notes by Elisabeth Guillot, Paris: Albin Michel.

Klemperer, Victor (2006/200), *The Language of the Third Reich: LTI – Lingua Tertii Imperii, A philologist's Notebook*, translated by Martin Brady, London: Continuum.

Lakoff, George and Mark Johnson (1999), *Philosophy in the Flesh: The Embodied Mind and its Challenge to Western Thought*, New York: Basic Books.

Lakoff, George (1987), *Women, Fire and Dangerous Things: What Categories Reveal about the Mind*, Chicago: University of Chicago Press.

Langham Brown, Roger (1967), *Wilhelm von Humboldt's Conception of Linguistic Relativity*, The Hague/Paris: Mouton.

Lee, Penny (1996), *The Whorf Theory Complex: A critical reconstruction*, Amsterdam/New York: John Benjamins Publishing Company.

Leech, Geoffrey [1974] (1990), *Semantics: The Study of Meaning*, 2nd edn, London: Penguin.

Lévi-Strauss, Claude (1961), *Race et Histoire*, Paris: Gonthier.

Littré, Emile (1962), *Dictionniare de la langue française*, France: Gallimard, Hachette.

Locke, John [1689] (1964), *An Essay Concerning Human Understanding*, Glasgow: Fontana, Collins.

Lucy, John A. [1992] (1996), *Language Diversity and Thought: A Reformulation of the Linguistic Relativity Hypothesis*, Cambridge: Cambridge University Press.

McArthur, Tom (1998), *The English Languages*, Cambridge: Cambridge University Press.

Malmkjaer, Kirsten (1991), *The Linguistics Encyclopedia*, London: Routledge.

Malotki, Ekkehart (1983), *Hopi Time: A linguistic analysis of the temporal concepts in the Hopi language*, Berlin: Mouton.

Manchester, L. Martin (1985), *The Philosophical Foundations of Humboldt's Linguistic Doctrines*, Amsterdam/Philadelphia: John Benjamins.

Meschonnic, Henri (1982), *Critique du rythme: anthropologie historique du langage*, Paris: Verdier.

Meschonnic, Henri (1985), *Les états de la poétique*, Paris: Presses Universitaires de France.

Meschonnic, Henri (1995a), *La Pensée dans la langue, Humboldt et après*, collected essays, ed. H. Meschonnic, Paris: Presses universitaires de Vincennes.

Meschonnic, Herni (1995b), *Politique du rythme: politique du sujet*, Paris: Verdier.

Meschonnic, Henri (1997), *De la langue française: Essai sur une clarté obscure*, Paris: Hachette.

Morier, Henri (1961), *Dictionnaire de poétique et de rhétorique*, Paris: Presses Universitaires de France.

Naugle, David K. (2002), *Worldview: The History of a Concept*, Grand Rapids: W. B. Eerdmans.

Nettle, Daniel, and Suzanne Romaine (2000), *Vanishing Voices: The Extinction of the World's Languages*, Oxford: Oxford University Press.

Picoche, Jacqueline (1994), *Le Robert dictionnaire étymologique du français*, Robert: Paris.

Plato (1961), *The Collected Dialogues*, ed. Edith Hamilton and Huntington Cairns, Princeton, NJ: Princeton University Press.

Plato (1968), *The Republic*, trans. with notes and an interpretive essay by Allan Bloom, New York: Basic Books.

Poldauf, Ivan (1986), *Česko-anglický slovník* [Czech-English Dictionary], 2nd edn, Prague: Státní pedagogoické nakladatelství.

Preminger, Alex, and N. T. V. F. Brogan (1993), *The Princeton Encyclopedia of Poetry and Poetics*, Princeton, NJ: Princeton University Press.

Rey, Alain [1992] (1998), *Dictionnaire historique de la langue française*, Robert: Paris.

Rey-Debove, Josette (2004), *Le Robert Brio, Analyse des mots et régularités du lexique*, Paris: Dictionnaires le Robert.

Russell, Bertrand [1946] (1979), *History of Western Philosophy*, London: Unwin Paperbacks.

Saint Augustine (1964a), 'De Musica', in Albert Hofstadter and Richard Kuhns (eds), *Philosophies of Art and Beauty: Selected Readings in Aesthetics from Plato to Heidegger*, Chicago: Chicago University Press, pp. 185–202.

Saint Augustine (1964b), *Les Confessions*, Paris: Garnier Frères Flammarion.

Salzmann, Zdenek (1999), *Language, Culture, and Society, An Introduction to Linguistic Anthropology*, 2nd edn, Boulder, CO: Westview Press.

Sapir, Edward [1921] (1949), *Language: An Introduction to the Study of Speech*, New York: Harcourt, Brace & World Inc.

Sapir, Edward [1949] (1985), *Selected Writings in Language, Culture, and Personality*, ed. David G. Mandelbaum, Berkeley: University of California Press.

Scruton, Roger [1982] (1996), *Kant*, Oxford: Oxford University Press.

Shakespeare, William (1976), *The Sonnets*, intro. by M. R. Ridley, London: Everyman's Library.

Shakespeare, William (1992), *The Illustrated Stratford Shakespeare*, London: Chancellor Press.

Simpson, Paul (1993), *Language, Ideology and Point of View*, London: Routledge.

Sire, James W. (2004), *Naming the Elephant: Worldview as a Concept*, Westmount, IL: InterVarsity Press.

Stamm, Anne (1999), *La parole est un monde*, Paris: Seuil.

Steiner, George (1975), *After Babel, Aspects of Language and Translation*, 2nd edn, Oxford: Oxford University Press.

Sweetser, E. (1990), *From Etymology to Pragmatics: Metaphorical and Cultural Aspects of Semantic Structure*, Cambridge: Cambridge University Press.

Taylor, John R. (1989), *Linguistic Categorization*, 3rd edn, Oxford: Oxford University Press.

Taylor, John R. (2002), *Cognitive Grammar*, Oxford: Oxford University Press.

Thomas, Linda, Shân Wareing, Ishthla Singh, Jean Stilwell Peccei, Joanna Thornborrow and Jason Jones [1999] (2004), *Language, Society and Power: An Introduction*, 2nd edn, London: Routledge.

Trabant, Jürgen (1992), *Humboldt ou le sens du langage*, Liège: Madarga.

Trabant, Jürgen [German edn 1990] (1999), *Traditions de Humboldt*, Paris: Maison des sciences de l'homme.

Vaňková, Irena (2001), *Obraz světa v jazyce* [The image of the world in language], Prague: Desktop Publishing FF UK.

Vinay, J.-P., and J. Darbelnet (1958), *Stylistique compare du français et de l'anglais*, Paris: Didier.

Whorf, Benjamin Lee [1956] (1984), *Language, Thought and Reality: Selected Writings*, ed. John B. Caroll, Cambridge, MA: MIT Press.

Wittgenstein, Ludwig (1969a), *The Blue and Brown Books*, 2nd edn, New York: Harper and Row.

Wittgenstein, Ludwig (1969b), *Schriften 1: Tractatus Logico-Philosophicus*, Frankfurt: Suhrkamp.

Wittgenstein, Ludwig (1984), *Werkausgabe*, vol. 1, Frankfurt am Main: Suhrkamp.

Wittgenstein, Ludwig [1922] (1993), *Tractatus logico-philosophicus*, French trans. by Gilles-Gaston Granger, Paris: Gallimard.

Wittgenstein, Ludwig [1953] (2001), *The Philosophical Investigations, The German Text with a Revised English Translation*, 3rd edn, Oxford: Blackwell.

Index